EARLY CHILDHOOD EDUCATION SERIES

Sharon Ryan, *Editor*

ADVISORY BOARD: *Celia Genishi, Doris Fromberg, Carrie Lobman, Rachel Theilheimer, Dominic Gullo, Amita Gupta, Beatrice Fennimore, Sue Grieshaber, Jackie Marsh, Mindy Blaise, Gail Yuen, Alice Honig, Betty Jones, Stephanie Feeney, Stacie G. Goffin, Beth Graue*

STEM Learning with Young Children:
Inquiry Teaching with Ramps and Pathways
SHELLY COUNSELL, LAWRENCE ESCALADA, ROSEMARY GEIKEN,
MELISSA SANDER, JILL UHLENBERG, BETH VAN MEETEREN,
SONIA YOSHIZAWA, & BETTY ZAN

Courageous Leadership in Early Childhood Education:
Taking a Stand for Social Justice
SUSI LONG, MARIANA SOUTO-MANNING,
& VIVIAN MARIA VASQUEZ, EDS.

Teaching Kindergarten:
Learner-Centered Classrooms for the 21st Century
JULIE DIAMOND, BETSY GROB, & FRETTA REITZES, EDS.

Healthy Learners: A Whole Child Approach
to Reducing Disparities in Early Education
ROBERT CROSNOE, CLAUDE BONAZZO, & NINA WU

The New Early Childhood Professional:
A Step-by-Step Guide to Overcoming Goliath
VALORA WASHINGTON, BRENDA GADSON, & KATHRYN L. AMEL

Eight Essential Techniques for Teaching with
Intention: What Makes Reggio and Other
Inspired Approaches Effective
ANN LEWIN-BENHAM

Teaching and Learning in a Diverse World, 4th Ed.
PATRICIA G. RAMSEY

In the Spirit of the Studio
Learning from the *Atelier* of Reggio Emilia, 2nd Ed.
LELLA GANDINI, LYNN HILL, LOUISE CADWELL,
& CHARLES SCHWALL, EDS.

Leading Anti-Bias Early Childhood Programs
A Guide for Change
LOUISE DERMAN-SPARKS, DEBBIE LEEKEENAN,
& JOHN NIMMO

Exploring Mathematics Through Play in the Early
Childhood Classroom
AMY NOELLE PARKS

Becoming Young Thinkers:
Deep Project Work in the Classroom
JUDY HARRIS HELM

The Early Years Matter: Education, Care, and the
Well-Being of Children, Birth to 8
MARILOU HYSON & HEATHER BIGGAR TOMLINSON

Thinking Critically About Environments for Young
Children: Bridging Theory and Practice
LISA P. KUH, ED.

Standing Up for Something Every Day:
Ethics and Justice in Early Childhood Classrooms
BEATRICE S. FENNIMORE

FirstSchool: Transforming PreK–3rd Grade for African
American, Latino, and Low-Income Children
SHARON RITCHIE & LAURA GUTMANN, EDS.

The States of Child Care: Building a Better System
SARA GABLE

Early Childhood Education for a New Era:
Leading for Our Profession
STACIE G. GOFFIN

Everyday Artists: Inquiry and Creativity in the
Early Childhood Classroom
DANA FRANTZ BENTLEY

Multicultural Teaching in the Early Childhood
Classroom: Approaches, Strategies, and Tools,
Preschool–2nd Grade
MARIANA SOUTO-MANNING

Inclusion in the Early Childhood Classroom:
What Makes a Difference?
SUSAN L. RECCHIA & YOON-JOO LEE

Language Building Blocks:
Essential Linguistics for Early Childhood Educators
ANITA PANDEY

Understanding the Language Development and Early
Education of Hispanic Children
EUGENE E. GARCÍA & ERMINDA H. GARCÍA

Moral Classrooms, Moral Children: Creating a
Constructivist Atmosphere in Early Education, 2nd Ed.
RHETA DEVRIES & BETTY ZAN

Defending Childhood:
Keeping the Promise of Early Education
BEVERLY FALK, ED.

...the Book: Using Literature to
... s

...ject
...tion

To look for other titles in this series, visit www.tcpress.com

(continued)

STEM Learning with Young Children

Inquiry Teaching with Ramps and Pathways

Shelly Counsell, Lawrence Escalada,
Rosemary Geiken, Melissa Sander,
Jill Uhlenberg, Beth Van Meeteren,
Sonia Yoshizawa, and Betty Zan

Regents' Center for Early Developmental Education at the
University of Northern Iowa

TEACHERS COLLEGE PRESS

TEACHERS COLLEGE | COLUMBIA UNIVERSITY
NEW YORK AND LONDON

Published by Teachers College Press, 1234 Amsterdam Avenue, New York, NY 10027

This material is based upon work supported by the National Science Foundation under Grant No. 0628082. Any opinions, findings, and conclusions or recommendations expressed in this material are those of the author(s) and do not necessarily reflect the views of the National Science Foundation.

Library of Congress Cataloging-in-Publication Data is available at loc.gov

Names: Counsel, Shelly.
Title: STEM learning with young children : inquiry teaching with ramps and
    pathways / Shelly Counsel [and seven others].
Description: New York, NY : Teachers College Press, [2016] I Series: Early
    childhood education series
Identifiers: LCCN 2015040141 I ISBN 9780807757499 (pbk. : alk. paper)
Subjects: LCSH: Science—Study and teaching (Early childhood)
Classification: LCC LB1139.5.S35 C68 2016 I DDC 372.35—dc23
LC record available at http://lccn.loc.gov/2015040141

ISBN 978-0-8077-5749-9 (paper)
ISBN 978-0-8077-7456-4 (ebook)

Printed on acid-free paper
Manufactured in the United States of America

23 22 21 20 19 18 17 16   8 7 6 5 4 3 2 1

1049771

Dedication

In Memory of Rheta DeVries

We dedicate this guide to the memory of our colleague, mentor, confidant, and friend, Rheta DeVries. Rheta's sharp intellect, lifelong commitment to constructivist theory and practice, and unrelenting passion for young children and families were in many ways the inspiration, catalyst, and driving force behind the Ramps and Pathways research and subsequent development of teaching practices described in this guide. Rheta's sheer determination to improve STEM teaching practices and learning outcomes with young children made this work possible.

We are forever in her debt. Ramps and Pathways will always remain as her lasting legacy.

Contents

Acknowledgments

This book represents a collaborative effort among researchers and teachers that dates back to the 1990s. Central to this effort is the Regents' Center for Early Developmental Education at the University of Northern Iowa (UNI). Under the direction of the late Rheta DeVries (1993–2006), Betty Zan (2007–2014), and Beth Van Meeteren (2014–present), the center has nurtured and supported constructivist, inquiry-based early childhood STEM education through professional development, curriculum development, and research. The Ramps and Pathways project was a direct outgrowth of one of the center's outreach efforts: the Iowa Teacher Practitioner Council. This council brought together preschool-through-2nd-grade teachers from across Iowa to collaborate with Regents' Center faculty at UNI on constructivist early education. Among other pursuits, these teachers actively sought to develop new methods and materials to support young children's understanding of force and motion through the investigation of inclined planes. When UNI opened an early childhood laboratory school (the Freeburg Early Childhood Program in Waterloo, Iowa), some of these teachers joined the faculty and continued this curriculum development work. We owe a huge debt of gratitude to all of these pioneering teachers.

We are also grateful to the National Science Foundation (NSF) for funding the curriculum development, pilot test, and national field test of the Ramps and Pathways project. We particularly acknowledge Robert Gibbs, our program officer at NSF. We could not have achieved what we did without his wisdom, guidance, and calm professionalism. During Robert's tenure at NSF, he was a fierce advocate for early childhood science education, and the field has benefited immensely from his work.

We could not have developed the Ramps and Pathways materials and resources without the teachers, assistant teachers, and children at the Freeburg Early Childhood Program: Christina Sales, Marilyn Luttenin, Kathy Thompson, and Sherri Peterson with 3-year-olds; Gwen Harmon, Jane Pearce, and Kristin Menninga with 4-year-olds; Sherice Hetrick-Ortman, Shirley Bruce, and Tara McPherson-Condon with kindergartners; and Beth Van Meeteren and Shari McGhee with 1st- and 2nd-graders. Melissa Sander explored ways to support children with special needs. Observing the collaboration and cooperation between these teachers and their students allowed us a window into what young children are capable of accomplishing in investigating force and motion if provided with the right support and materials.

We gratefully acknowledge the contributions and support of Regents' Center staff Catherine Richey, Kathryn Thompson, Seth Vickers, and Theresa Johnson, and UNI students Alison Gilchrist and Kelsey Knebel. We could not have completed the field test without the contributions of our site facilitators: Carolyn Black and Karen Capo in Houston, Texas; Averee Kirkland-Patton and Stephanie Langley in Birmingham, Alabama; and Sally Peña in Pocatello, Idaho.

We are indebted to the teachers who participated in the Iowa pilot study and the teachers in Idaho, Alabama, and Texas who participated in the field test. The Ramps and Pathways project was unconventional in the realm of curriculum development. It was never designed to be a curriculum in the traditional sense of the word, with clearly defined lessons, scripted interactions, and a scope and sequence. Rather, it was (and is) an approach to STEM that relies on active co-construction between teachers and children. The teachers' willingness to be experimental is a testimony to their dedication and commitment to early STEM education. The preschool-through-2nd-grade teachers in southeast Idaho during the 2008–2009 field site testing provided important insights and lived experiences that are used to guide and support R&P activities and practices with the full range of learners within diverse learning communities, as discussed in Chapter 5. These teachers' testimonials lend additional credence to the design and implementation of STEM professional development and the creation of STEM cultures of practice using R&P in early childhood and primary grade settings, as described in Chapter 8.

Finally, we want to express our sincere gratitude to the editors, Marie Ellen Larcada and Sarah Biondello at Teachers College Press, for their tireless efforts to shepherd this book into publication.

Preface

This guide represents the collective experience and combined expertise of the individual authors. Each had a formal role or roles on the project, yet these roles do not begin to describe the many and varied ways in which each person contributed to and shaped the project. What each author could accomplish alone does not equal what has been achieved together. As a team, we have always insisted that this work is greater and far more important than any individual or set of contributions. For this reason, the team decided that the most equitable approach is to list the authors alphabetically.

Each chapter in the guide is further strengthened by the interconnected ideas, concepts, and information presented. The end result is a comprehensive guide designed to help early childhood educators transform STEM teaching and improve learner outcomes using Ramps and Pathways with the full range of young children in a variety of educational settings.

Why STEM?
Why Early Childhood?
Why Now?

Betty Zan

In a field known for embracing "hot topics," perhaps no topic in education has received as much press as STEM (science, technology, engineering, and math). In recent years, much of the conversation about science education has shifted to STEM—a term that is *not* simply the sum of the four disciplines as the acronym suggests. Rather, STEM education integrates these four disciplines into an interdisciplinary approach. However, many early childhood educators do not fully grasp the relevance of this shift and how it can guide and inform subsequent practice with young children.

In this introduction, I start by defining and explaining each content area (science, technology, engineering, and mathematics) in relation to young children and discussing why it is important for early childhood educators to use an interdisciplinary approach. Next, I cite current research to support this guide's assertion that STEM experiences begin at birth as children observe and engage with their surroundings, and therefore that formal STEM education must begin in the early years. I address the urgency that this country faces in ensuring that all its citizens are STEM literate. Finally, I outline the organizational structure of this guide.

DEFINITIONS

Any discussion of STEM teaching and learning must begin with the dictionary definition of each of the STEM disciplines, such as these, taken from *Merriam-Webster Dictionary* (www.merriam-webster.com):

> *Science:* knowledge about or study of the natural world based on facts learned through experiments and observation

Technology: the use of science in industry, engineering, etc., to invent useful things or to solve problems

Engineering: the work of designing and creating large structures or new products or systems by using scientific methods

Mathematics: the science of numbers and their operations, interrelations, combinations, generalizations, and abstractions and of space configurations and their structure, measurement, transformations, and generalizations

Please note that these definitions alone may not help early educators figure out how best to teach STEM content to young children. The subsequent chapters in this guide are designed to provide the necessary details and examples to help early educators figure out how to teach STEM content using Ramps and Pathways (R&P).

Science

The dictionary definition of *science* stresses that it consists of knowledge about or the study of the natural world, and that it is based on close observation and experimentation. However, this is not how science has traditionally been taught in our schools. More often, science instruction has centered on memorizing terms and following step-by-step instructions to find the predetermined answer to a question posed by the teacher. Although this tightly controlled exercise is often labeled an experiment, it lacks a key element of an experiment: learner involvement.

Teachers (myself included, unfortunately) often tend to teach in the same way we have been taught. Listening to early educators across the country, I have learned that few educators had opportunities in their own schooling to actually think about a question that piqued their curiosity, to ponder how they might explore the question further, and then to design and conduct an investigation to figure it out. And yet, this is what young children independently do when they are in unstructured settings. For example, think about a child swinging on a standard playground swing. The child quickly learns how to pump his or her legs to cause the swing to go higher. Soon the child wonders whether pumping his or her legs can make the swing go all the way up and around the crossbar (one complete revolution). So the child pumps harder and harder, replicating his or her actions over days and weeks, until he or she finally concludes that it is not possible. This represents the child's own investigation, designed to answer the child's own question. It marks the beginnings of experimentation, and it *is* science. Therefore, we recommend a practical definition of science for early educators: Science is the observation and investigation of the natural world and how it works.

DEFINITIONS FOR EARLY EDUCATORS

Educators can use the following definitions to help guide, facilitate, and support STEM teaching and learning with young children:

Science: investigation of the natural world and how it works
Technology: any human modification of the natural world
Engineering: an approach to designing and creating the human-made world
Mathematics: the study of number, quantity, and space

Technology

The dictionary definition of *technology* stresses the use of science "in industry, engineering, etc." I would suggest that the *et cetera* is the most interesting part of this definition. Broadly, technology is anything that is invented to meet a human need or want. It is the human-made world. The National Assessment of Educational Progress (NAEP)'s framework for technology and engineering literacy adopted the definition of technology offered by the National Academy of Engineering: "any modification of the natural world made to fulfill human needs or desires" (Gamire & Pearson, 2006, p. 1). The International Technology and Engineering Educators Association (ITEEA; 2007) standards state that "Technology has been going on since humans first formed a blade from a piece of flint, harnessed fire, or dragged a sharp stick across the ground to create a furrow for planting seeds" (p. 2).

Consider the technology used to create this guide. Paper and ink were critical human inventions that enabled humans to record information they wanted to be able to retrieve. If you are reading this on a digital device, you are enjoying a new form of technology that is no less revolutionary than the printing press was centuries ago. You are probably sitting on a piece of furniture (a technology far superior to sitting on the hard ground), and perhaps you are drinking something out of a cup (a technology more efficient than cupping one's hands to hold a liquid).

My purpose in pointing out these simple forms of technology is to combat the popular (but limited) understanding of technology as electronics, computers, digital media, and the like. Certainly, these are all forms of technology. But technology has always been about solving problems and addressing human wants and needs. Therefore, we recommend a practical definition of *technology* for early educators: any human modification of the natural world.

One way young children learn about technology is by becoming aware of the many ways humans use technology to improve their daily lives. Traffic signals protect lives by regulating the flow of traffic. Microwave ovens heat up snacks quickly and efficiently. Hand magnifying lenses enable a child to see an insect's legs in minute detail. Balance scales make it possible to compare weights and determine which ball is heavier. All these examples illustrate ways that children can experience and use technology to address individual wants and needs in daily life. But young children are not simply users of technology; they can also invent their own technology. When children use a large block to stand on to reach a higher counter, or create a structure to house their doll or stuffed animal, they are designing technology.

Engineering

The dictionary definitions of *engineering* and *technology* are very similar. One way to keep these two disciplines distinct is to think of technology as "the human-made world," and engineering as "designing and creating" the human-made world. The National Research Council (NRC, 2009) concurs, defining engineering as "a systematic and often iterative approach to designing objects, processes, and systems to meet human needs and wants" (p. 49). Therefore, we recommend a practical definition of engineering for early educators: an approach to designing and creating the human-made world.

Many different models of the design process exist, although all share certain components: identifying a problem, brainstorming possible solutions, designing and building a solution, testing and evaluating it, improving it, and communicating results. These are discussed in more detail in Chapter 6.

Although there are many different branches of engineering, four main branches are generally recognized: mechanical, chemical, electrical, and civil. The branch that is perhaps most suited to preschoolers is mechanical engineering, because it involves processes that children can observe and manipulate directly. For example, when children push down on one end of a lever, they can observe the other end going up immediately. When they play with gears, they can see that when one gear turns clockwise, the adjoining gear turns counterclockwise.

Mathematics

Typically, in early childhood, mathematics is equated with number and quantity, and special emphasis is placed on learning how to count. Without discounting the importance of counting, I must point out that the field of mathematics consists of much more than just number and quantity. The National Council of Teachers of Mathematics (NCTM) breaks down mathematics content into five content standards: number and operations, algebra, geometry, measurement, and data analysis and probability.

MATHEMATICS CONTENT STANDARDS (FROM NCTM, 2000)

Number and operations: understanding numbers, ways of representing numbers, relationships among numbers, and number systems; understanding the meanings of operations and how they relate to one another; computing fluently and making reasonable estimates

Algebra: understanding patterns, relations, and functions; representing and analyzing mathematical situations and structures using algebraic symbols; using mathematical models to represent and understand quantitative relationships; and analyzing change in various contexts

Geometry: analyzing characteristics and properties of 2- and 3-dimensional geometric shapes and developing mathematical arguments about geometric relationships; specifying locations and describing spatial relationships using coordinate geometry and other representational systems; applying transformations and using symmetry to analyze mathematical situations; using visualization, spatial reasoning, and geometric modeling to solve problems

Measurement: understanding measurable attributes of objects and the units, systems, and processes of measurement; applying appropriate techniques, tools, and formulas to determine measurements

Data Analysis and Probability: formulating questions that can be addressed with data and collecting, organizing, and displaying relevant data to answer them; selecting and using appropriate statistical methods to analyze data; developing and evaluating inferences and predictions that are based on data; understanding and applying basic concepts of probability

---

Mathematics is also about processes, and the NCTM identifies four process standards: problem solving, reasoning and proof, communication, and connection. These standards cover a great deal of content. For the purposes of early education, we adopt a somewhat simpler definition of mathematics: the study of number, quantity, and space.

Mathematics has been called the "language of science" (the phrase may have originated with Galileo in 1623; today, a Google search of the phrase turns up more than 100,000 hits). To illustrate, imagine trying to describe the world (a central aspect of science) without using mathematical language. The world exists in three-dimensional space, and therefore must be described and mapped in spatial terms. Measurement is a critical component of describing anything. How else, besides using measurement-related words (such as *large* and *small*, *heavy* and *light*) would one distinguish between, say, a mouse and an elephant? And whenever one begins to measure anything, counting units of measure quickly comes into play.

Another critical aspect of science is the ability to make predictions about the world. How can an individual predict anything without first collecting data and analyzing patterns? Think of the simple act of watering houseplants. Over time, a plant owner observes the results of different amounts of water and different frequencies of watering, until he or she begins to detect patterns of results (leaves shrivel or turn yellow, or the plant thrives). This is data analysis. Data analysis and algebra are central to scientific prediction, and all five of the content strands are essential to engaging in science.

WHY STEM?

As stated earlier, STEM is not simply the sum of its four disciplines. Rather, it is an interdisciplinary approach that seamlessly integrates all four of the component disciplines. Integral to STEM education is the provision of opportunities for children to have direct experiences and engage in real-world problems.

One reason why this integration works is quite simply that all four disciplines share the same process: problem solving. The problem may be related to understanding something that is puzzling (for example, why are there so many worms on the sidewalk after a spring rain?). The problem may be related to finding a practical solution to a vexing situation (for example, how can we design and build a bird feeder that the squirrels won't raid?). Or the problem may be mathematical in nature (for example, how many pizzas do we need to purchase for the party so that everyone will get two slices?). In every instance, problem solving is central.

The interdisciplinary approach is also evident in the recently released *Next Generation Science Standards* (NGSS; NRC, 2013), particularly within the scientific and engineering practices. This explicit framework includes both scientific and engineering practices as well as mathematics, computational thinking, and data analysis.

WHY EARLY CHILDHOOD?

Young children are capable of engaging in serious STEM investigations when they are guided by skilled and knowledgeable teachers. However, many early childhood teachers lack sufficient STEM content knowledge and report feeling unprepared to teach STEM content (Akerson, 2004;

**SCIENTIFIC AND ENGINEERING PRACTICES (FROM THE NEXT
GENERATION SCIENCE STANDARDS [NRC, 2013])**

1. Asking questions (science) and defining problems (engineering)
2. Developing and using models
3. Planning and carrying out investigations
4. Analyzing and interpreting data
5. Using mathematics and computational thinking
6. Constructing explanations (science) and designing solutions
   (engineering)
7. Engaging in argument from evidence
8. Obtaining, evaluating, and communicating information

Greenfield et al., 2009; Kallery & Psillos, 2001; National Research Council, 2007; Sandholtz & Ringstaff, 2011; Wenner, 1993; Yasar, Baker, Robinson-Kurpius, Krause, & Roberts, 2006). Additionally, the National Research Council's foundational work, *Taking Science to School* (2007), reports that schools and educators consistently underestimate young children's abilities. Opportunities to introduce young children to important STEM concepts and processes are being missed every day because teachers do not provide activities that challenge children to think about and engage with STEM content beyond memorizing isolated facts.

STEM is also important because of the attitudes that it fosters. Early childhood offers opportunities to develop positive attitudes toward STEM that will serve all children well throughout their school careers. By engaging in STEM experiences, children have opportunities to develop habits and behaviors that will serve them well in academic achievement in all domains. During the early years, children are beginning to develop self-control, memory, attention, and the ability to make intentional plans with others. These executive functions, considered foundational for problem solving, have been found to improve the development of later academic skills (Brock, Rimm-Kaufman, Nathanson, & Grimm, 2009; Diamond, Barnett, Thomas, & Munro, 2007). Engineering habits of mind (Katehi, Pearson, & Feder, 2009), which include creativity, problem solving, and analytical skills, are valuable not only for engineering but for all aspects of life and can easily begin to be nurtured in early childhood.

Consider approaches to learning (AtL), a domain of early childhood education considered a school readiness area by the U.S. Department of Health and Human Services, as seen by its inclusion in the *Head Start Child Development and Early Learning Framework* (Office of Head Start, 2011). AtL is defined as the attitudes and dispositions that influence all learning, which include curiosity, persistence, inventiveness, sustained attention, flexibility, and desire for a challenge. These dispositions are promoted as children engage in planned STEM learning experiences (Van Meeteren & Zan, 2010). An integrated approach using active engagement with young children not only increases learning across the four STEM disciplines, but also promotes children's overall development across all domains (cognitive, language, social–emotional, and motor).

Finally, research is beginning to show that early exposure to STEM experiences is critical to fostering and sustaining student participation, interest, and agency in engineering and science (Capobianco, Yu, & French, 2014; Varelas, Kane, & Wylie, 2011). As a nation, we cannot afford to shut down children's interest in STEM for 4 years (pre-K through 2nd grade) to focus primarily on literacy and math, and expect 3rd- and 4th-graders to suddenly be interested and engaged in STEM. Our children need the benefit of an integrated curriculum that allows them to capitalize on the synergy among the disciplines.

WHY NOW?

This country is facing a crisis in the STEM field. Student achievement in STEM is low. Students express little interest in STEM fields, and few students choose to study STEM at the college level or pursue STEM careers after high school (Katehi, Pearson, & Feder, 2009). According to the President's Council of Advisors on Science and Technology (PCAST, 2010), "STEM education will determine whether the United States will remain a leader among nations and whether we will be able to solve immense challenges in such areas as energy, health, environmental protection, and national security." To be able to do this, our country needs all of its citizens to be STEM literate: people who understand and use STEM information and habits of mind in their daily lives, in their decisionmaking, and in their voting. We need a workforce that is STEM capable and ready to take on the jobs of the 21st century. We urgently need students to enter into the STEM pipeline, to become the future STEM teachers who prepare and inspire the next generation of science learners and the future STEM experts who can develop new knowledge and create new solutions to the world's problems.

Predictions made in *Rising Above the Gathering Storm* (National Academy of Sciences, 2007) suggested that our country would need 10,000 new STEM teachers every year to replace those who are about to retire in order to keep up with the growing demand. PCAST issued a report in 2010 predicting that over the next decade, the United States would need approximately a million more STEM professionals than it is currently producing.

If early childhood educators hope to prepare and inspire young children to become the STEM workforce leaders of the future, they must start now. The Ramps and Pathways project, activities, and materials described in this guide represent an interdisciplinary approach to STEM for young children that is rich in possibilities for extended experiences with STEM content and processes.

ORGANIZATION OF THIS BOOK

This guide is a collaborative effort of the many professionals who worked on the Ramps and Pathways research project. It is our sincere hope that this guide will contribute to early childhood teachers' growing competence and confidence related to STEM education.

Chapter 1 addresses the question: Why provide ramp activities in the classroom setting? Chapter 2 answers practical questions related to how best to prepare the classroom setting and children for ramp activities. Chapter 3 provides much-needed physics content that is fundamental to ramp exploration and investigation. Chapter 4 focuses on issues and concepts related to communication and language during ramp activities. Chapter 5 explores how ramps can be implemented to promote STEM learning and development for the full range of learners, including children with disabilities, children identified as gifted and talented, and dual-language learners. Chapter 6 provides practical recommendations for integrating ramps into any classroom literacy program. Chapter 7 addresses the important issue of assessment. Finally, Chapter 8 explores how to support teachers through professional development efforts. Altogether, this comprehensive guide provides essential information designed to help educators further expand, enhance, and enrich any early childhood classroom or school STEM curriculum using R&P.

CHAPTER 1

Why Use Ramps and Pathways?

Betty Zan

Ramps and Pathways (R&P) is a STEM-based approach to engaging young children in inquiry, problem solving, and active investigation of force and motion through the use of inclined planes and the movement of objects. R&P is not a curriculum in the traditional sense of a fixed set of lessons that occur in a particular order. Rather, it is an approach to designing experiences that engage young children in creating and building ramp structures to move objects. These experiences actively engage children in engineering design and scientific inquiry. As children have ideas about the structures they want to build and imagine the path of the object they want to move, they also utilize spatial thinking, an essential mathematical objective often ignored in early childhood, but essential in STEM thinking, as well as counting, measuring and comparing, and early data analysis.

The authors of this book believe that in addition to scientific and mathematical benefits, engaging in R&P activities has socioemotional benefits as well. Consider this story, told by Shari McGhee, an assistant teacher in a 1st-grade classroom:

Melaina came to us a month into 1st grade, seemingly terrified of school, withdrawn to the point of taking refuge under a table in tears. I knew that my teaching partner and I needed to find a way to gain her trust. Melaina spent most of her first weeks in our classroom in self-imposed isolation, crying and physically clinging to us, unable or unwilling to verbalize what she was feeling. We tried to get her to write down what she was feeling in her journal, but she spent the majority of journal time crying, fearful of writing down words that were misspelled, despite our assurances that writing was a process and she only needed to get the sounds down to read it back. We didn't realize it at the time but now that I look back, Melaina was very fortunate to be in a classroom like ours. Our classroom was nontraditional. Most of the curriculum was hands-on. We had open-ended centers and areas for learning rather than individual desks. One of these centers was Ramps and Pathways.

I decided to start to work on developing a relationship with Melaina in Ramps and Pathways for several reasons. First, Ramps and Pathways allows children to work alone or in groups. It is the child's choice. Melaina seemed fearful of all relationships (with adults or children), and the Ramps center allowed her the privacy she needed. Second, Ramps and Pathways does not demand verbal or written responses for a child to feel successful. I began to build next to Melaina and talked to myself as I built, providing a model for Melaina as to how I was thinking. Occasionally, I would stop and ask myself a question. Within days, Melaina began to answer my questions with her actions as she released marbles on the ramp structures she built independently using varied sizes of wooden cove molding sections. Gradually, she became comfortable having a conversation with me. I watched how her self-confidence began to grow as she challenged herself with the ramps. She began like most beginning builders and first laid out the ramps in a straight line. Then she took on new challenges, such as making the marble turn corners. I watched her critical thinking processes as well as her confidence improve.

After a couple of months, Melaina began to migrate to Ramps and Pathways without me by her side. One morning as I was working in another part of the classroom, Melaina grabbed my hand and said, "Come and see what I did!" I walked over to Ramps and Pathways to find she had taken on the challenge of doing a zigzag ramp system. Prior to this attempt, Melaina had observed other children's unsuccessful attempts to build zigzag structures. In this complex system, each ramp had to be at a slight incline to slow the marble's speed in order to negotiate each sharp turn. Each section had to work in concert with the next, with careful attention to a patterned decrease in elevation from start to end. Melaina's execution was not only right on mathematically, but her placement of the blocks was visually appealing as well. I watched as she placed the marble at the top of her structure. As it rolled down the first ramp, it approached the first block embankment. It ricocheted to the next ramp and continued along each ramp section, until it reached the end of the last ramp. Melaina beamed with confidence as I embraced and congratulated her, sharing her moment of triumph.

The more Melaina was successful, the more she initiated conversations as she worked. As a result, her vocabulary increased and her confidence grew to a level where she started to help the other kids with challenges they encountered that she had already mastered. It was awesome to see how comfortable she became working with ramps and eventually in all the areas in our classroom. This girl was growing into a happy, confident child, totally different from the girl who first came to us.

My teaching partner and I believe Melaina was able to transition into a powerful learner in part because of what took place in the Ramps center that year. Today, I often get the opportunity to see Melaina as I shop for groceries. This formerly scared 1st-grader now stands taller than me, is confident, and wears a big smile. She always has a hug for me, and I for her.

My R&P colleagues and I have found that when R&P materials (pieces of wooden cove molding that can be used as inclined planes) are placed in classrooms by teachers who are truly interested in exploring force and motion with children, children are inspired by the materials and spend long periods of time building increasingly more complex ramp structures. Uninformed observers may be tempted to dismiss children's investigations as mere "play," devoid of educational content. Nothing could be further from the truth! In this chapter, my aim is twofold: first, to show you that R&P can be a valuable component of your STEM curriculum, and second, to arm you with information to provide to administrators and/or supervisors, parents, and other stakeholders that justifies R&P's place in quality STEM curricula.

Our advocacy of R&P activities is based on an extensive body of early childhood research and theory. This theoretical framework led us to develop the Inquiry Teaching Model (ITM; see Figure 1.1 in this chapter) that guides our recommendations about teaching.

Finally, I link R&P to science education standards that reflect consensus in the field of science education concerning what should be taught in science and how. These are discussed below.

RESEARCH AND THEORETICAL FOUNDATION
FOR RAMPS AND PATHWAYS

From birth, children constantly explore their environment in order to make sense of it. The extensive research of Jean Piaget (1948/1960, 1971/1974) into how children come to know what they know demonstrates powerfully that children construct knowledge of the physical world through exploring, experimenting, and forming early beliefs (or theories) about how the world works (Karmiloff-Smith & Inhelder, 1974). Even though young children's beliefs may be incorrect from a purely scientific perspective, those beliefs and ideas represent their best efforts to make sense of their surroundings. Young children devote a great deal of mental energy to thinking about what they observe in the world around them.

Taking Science to School (National Research Council, 2007) summarizes decades of research demonstrating that young children's ability to reason scientifically is vastly underestimated, especially in schools. Our work with young children on R&P activities leads us to concur. One reason for this underestimation may stem from different interpretations of what counts as scientific knowledge. Randall Knight (2004), a physics education researcher, identifies three categories of physics knowledge: (1) factual knowledge, (2) conceptual knowledge, and (3) procedural knowledge. He defines *factual* knowledge as knowledge of specific events and situations. Some factual knowledge we obtain directly through experience (for example, our understanding that when a ball is released at the top of an incline, it will roll down). Most of us learned in school that two objects of different weights dropped from the same height will land at the same time. However (and this is huge), air resistance must be eliminated as a variable. For most of us, when we first encountered this concept, we found it counterintuitive, and we had difficulty believing it. How many of us have actually had the opportunity to witness this sort of experiment in such a form that we were convinced of it? It is a difficult experiment to construct. The objects must be of exactly the same size and shape; they must be dropped at exactly the same time (try that with children); and the observers must be able to tell that they landed at the same time. I doubt many of us have seen this concept demonstrated satisfactorily more than once (if at all). It generally takes most learners, adults and children, multiple opportunities to experience a given phenomenon before they are willing to change strongly held beliefs.

Some factual knowledge is accepted on the basis of authority, rather than experience. The learner accepts it as factual because the learner believes what the authority figure tells him or her. A problem with knowledge that rests solely on authority is that we generally do not completely understand or believe it, in part because of our lack of direct experience ("seeing is believing"). Gaining experience through active experimentation can change the basis of factual knowledge from authority to direct experience (and reinforce that knowledge as a new strongly held belief based on actual observation). However, a problem in teaching science is that sometimes direct experiences with physical phenomena are not possible (due to time, space, or budgetary constraints). For example, Newton's First Law, as it applies to objects in motion, states that objects will remain in motion in the same direction and at the same speed, unless acted on by a force. One reason why this law is so difficult for some people to understand and accept is that it is only true in a non-friction environment. Most people have never had the opportunity to see objects moving in such an environment. It is an example of factual knowledge that is accepted on authority, without direct experience, and is not necessarily understood. As children get older, virtual experiences can sometimes substitute for actual experiences, but for young children, there is no substitute for real experiences.

Knight defines *conceptual* knowledge as knowledge of physical principles that bring many pieces of factual knowledge together into a unified whole. When children bring together various pieces of knowledge and try to connect them, they are engaged in concept development. One common misinterpretation of Piaget's stages of cognitive development is that young children do not (or cannot) engage with conceptual knowledge. In fact, young children do this all the time. For example, consider the common preschool activity in which children place objects in a tub of water and observe whether the objects sink or float. Young children frequently come up with explanations for why some objects sink while others float, such as that heavy objects sink and light objects float. This is incorrect, but it is an example of a child's attempt to pull together pieces of factual knowledge and unify them into a concept that can be used to explain and predict events. Both factual and conceptual knowledge held by individuals (both children and adults) may be partially or entirely incorrect.

Knight defines *procedural* knowledge as knowledge of how to apply factual and/or conceptual knowledge to specific problem-solving situations—that is, knowing how to use what you know to solve or figure something out. Children are great at this, having had years of experience exploring and examining their physical environment in order to come up with ideas about how the world works, and using their knowledge of how the world works to make something interesting happen. For example, when faced with the challenge of building a ramp structure that includes a right angle, children will often figure out how to place a block so that the marble strikes the block, bounces off the block, and lands on the next ramp segment, thus turning the corner. Although children do not possess specific knowledge about *why* collisions change the motion of objects, they can learn to make adjustments in the position of the blocks and ramps in order to get the marble to move in the direction they want.

In the same way that children organize bits and pieces of factual knowledge into concepts, so too do they tend to organize their procedural knowledge into "practical" theories about the physical world. Some of these theories are inaccurate by current scientific standards; however, these strongly held beliefs (sometimes referred to by science educators as misconceptions, preconceptions, alternative conceptions, or naïve ideas) are entrenched and resistant to change. It is important to emphasize that developing conceptual understanding of basic physics ideas (such as the law of inertia) is not a direct goal of R&P. Rather, the goals are for children to develop factual and procedural knowledge (for example, spherical objects roll downhill; objects gain speed as they roll downhill; objects can be stopped by placing an obstacle in their path) based on their direct experiences and investigations using R&P.

Ongoing experiences using R&P enable children to organize their factual knowledge into systems that serve as the early foundation for the later development of conceptual knowledge. The R&P materials and activities are designed to give young children practical experiences that help them learn how to "do" (and actively experience) STEM. These activities will lay the foundation for children's later active construction of ideas and explanations related to the laws of force and motion as recommended by the *Next Generation Science Standards* (NRC, 2013).

THE INQUIRY TEACHING MODEL

Science instruction for young children is known to be more effective when concepts are introduced within the context of concrete experiences. McDermott (1991) states that physics ideas should be taught as a process of inquiry, rather than as an unchanging body of knowledge. Students at an early age can begin to focus on the processes of doing investigations, develop the ability to ask scientific questions, and investigate aspects of the world around them, all of which can eventually lead them to use their observations to construct reasonable explanations for questions posed at a later age (NRC, 1996). It is this recognition of the central role that inquiry plays in learning that led us to develop the Inquiry Teaching Model (ITM) (see Figure 1.1) as a means of helping teachers develop, plan, implement, and evaluate STEM instructional experiences. This model is grounded in both early childhood and science education learning theories. Although this framework can be helpful in teaching learners of any age, I limit the discussion here to children in the preschool through 2nd-grade age range (3–8 years). I want to stress

Figure 1.1. Inquiry Teaching Model (ITM)

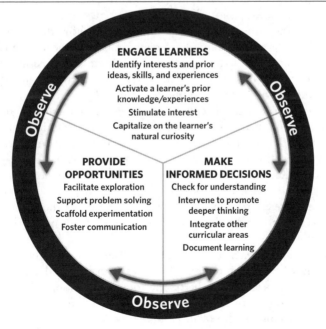

that this is not a learning cycle. It is a framework for talking about what teachers can do to support children's inquiry and advance children's learning. Although each section of the model (Engage Learners, Provide Opportunities, and Make Informed Decisions) is discussed separately, in practice, teachers move among them continually in a nonlinear manner. The arrows on the chart are bidirectional to indicate this. I also want to stress that everything the teacher does to support children's inquiry learning is fundamentally guided and informed by one primary activity: child observation.

Engage Learners

Engaged learners invest more mental energy in learning than unengaged learners. Fortunately, when inquiry is the central teaching approach, children become actively engaged in the learning process. Engaging children involves identifying and stimulating children's interests, activating their prior knowledge and experiences, and capitalizing on their natural curiosity (DeVries & Kohlberg, 1987/1990).

Tapping into children's individual interests is central to the constructivist approach in general, and particularly helpful within the domain of science. The *Benchmarks for Science Literacy* (AAAS, 1993) recommend that "Students should be actively involved in exploring phenomena that interest them both in and out of class" (p. 10). One way of thinking about the importance of interest is to think about something that interests you. Chances are, you know a great deal about it. Quilters, for example, know a lot about geometry. Cooks know a lot about how different ingredients taste, smell, and feel, how they interact with one another, and how they react to heat and cold. Gardeners know a lot about plants, sunlight, weather, and insects.

Now consider what happens when you are not interested in something. For example, what happens when you are required to attend a work-related meeting that you find boring and uninteresting? If you are like most adults, you force yourself to listen, because you recognize that if you do not, something bad could happen (such as missing out on important information that you need in order to complete job tasks accurately). Adults are capable of focusing their attention on something that does not particularly interest them because they can think beyond their short-term experience of being bored to the long-term reasons why they need to pay attention and the potential negative consequences if they don't. However, the ability to direct attention to something that holds little or no interest for us develops gradually over time.

Probably every teacher of young children can describe an incident where a child who was not interested in group time proceeded to disrupt the class by doing something that he or she found interesting (such as playing with the Velcro on his or her shoes or talking to a child nearby). Although it is true that young children can be made to *do* certain actions or follow specified directions (such as completing a worksheet or gluing pasta to construction paper), they cannot be forced to actually *think* about something deeply if the topic does not interest them. And it is children's thinking, much more than their actions, that is central to an inquiry-based approach to science education. According to Piaget (1981), interest is the fuel that drives the engine of mental activity.

If interest is the fuel of mental activity, then equilibration is the motor. In Piaget's theory, all learning is driven by a deep-seated need to achieve and maintain an inner state that he calls equilibrium. According to Piaget (1978), when we are faced with something new that we have never experienced before, we experience surprise, confusion, or contradiction that disturbs, if even mildly, our inner state of equilibrium. In order to make sense of the new experience or information, we draw on all of our prior knowledge to see how the new experience and subsequent information fit within our existing knowledge. If new information connects easily to prior knowledge, then we are satisfied. However, if we cannot connect the new information to something we already know, then the new information leads us to an inner state of disturbance—Piaget calls this disequilibrium—that drives us to continue thinking about it. Once we are able to make sense of it, we are then able to return to a state of equilibrium.

According to the theory of equilibration, it is our desire and need to resolve disturbances in our inner state of equilibrium that drives learning. This is why, when teachers begin a new unit of study, they first determine what children already know. Assessing children's prior knowledge requires close observation and careful listening. The longstanding practice of completing a K-W-L chart (K-W-L stands for what children already *know* [K], what they *want* to know [W], and revisited later, what they have *learned* [L]) at the beginning and end of a unit of study reflects this recognition of the importance of building on children's foundation of existing knowledge. Unless teachers know about children's ideas and where they come from, they will not be able to provide appropriate experiences and intervene in ways that support children's learning.

Young children are naturally curious. Observant teachers capitalize on using children's curiosity to support thinking and inquiry. Young children generally love to make something interesting happen, and frequently, what they make happen involves physical science concepts and relationships. Children stack blocks higher and higher, roll toy cars or pebbles down the playground slide, mix every color of paint available, pour water from one container to another, and on and on. Young children's curiosity is limited only by the experiences they are allowed. If they never experience something, they can't be curious about it. One way teachers can engage children's thinking is by introducing them to phenomena that will spark their curiosity. Teachers can also continue to observe children for indications that their interest is beginning to wane and, when this happens, take steps to pique it again. For example, teachers can draw attention to a previously unnoticed element of an activity, add a new material that acts somewhat differently, or suggest a new way of using the materials. Throughout a unit of instruction of any length, it is critical that teachers continue to observe and reassess whether children appear interested and how learners are actively engaged in exploring how the world works.

Provide Opportunities

Babies begin very early in life exploring the world in order to figure out how it works. Most of the time, this looks like play. Early education has a long tradition of recognizing the role of young children's play in the process of learning and development. During play, children learn about the properties of materials and objects, identify variables, notice patterns, and begin to construct cause-and-effect relationships. Exploration provides children with a common base of experiences from which teachers can draw in designing more in-depth investigations to specifically highlight particular concepts, skills, and processes that teachers want to introduce to children.

Facilitating children's active exploration of the physical world involves making adequate space and materials available to children, giving children enough time to explore, and creating a safe environment in which exploration is valued and nurtured. It also involves observing children to make sure that they know how to play and explore. Sometimes how to play appropriately with specific materials needs to be modeled directly for certain children. The role of the teacher is primarily that of a facilitator: setting up the environment, observing children, and providing assistance when needed.

Facilitating children's active exploration of the world also involves supporting children in posing and solving problems for themselves. When children are given interesting, open-ended materials and the space and time to explore them, they frequently begin to identify problems and seek solutions. For example, we have found that when children create ramp structures in the block area with cove molding, they inevitably reach the point where they want to make the marble turn a corner. Solving this problem is complex, but not too complex for young children to solve, and we have seen children spend extended periods of time trying to figure it out.

As children's exploratory play evolves, the teacher's role also evolves. As teachers observe children and determine what they are investigating, they can support those investigations through their provision of additional materials and the removal of others. Decisions about which materials to make available to children requires close observation in order to determine which variables children are noticing and manipulating. Children in the 2nd grade and younger generally do not understand the concept of a "fair test" in science, and do not know how to control variables (or even why they would need to). For this reason, they cannot be said to engage in true experimentation. However, teachers can scaffold this emerging ability by controlling some variables for children, so that children can begin to construct cause-and-effect relationships.

If too many variables are presented to children, they have difficulty noticing patterns in the ways the materials react. For example, if the teacher notices that children are investigating the effects of varying the height of the ramp, the teacher might make sure that all the marbles are the same size and weight and made of the same material. This way, children will be less likely to become confused by having many different types of marbles that might also affect the distance the marble travels, and they can focus more easily on the effects of changing the height.

Teachers also support children's learning through their use of language. They may use comparison words such as *higher, lower, longer, shorter, faster,* and *slower* to draw children's attention to differences in how the ramp structure is constructed and how the marble moves on the ramp. They introduce spatial language to encourage spatial visualization such as *in front of, next to, on top of.* They also foster children's communication about what they have figured out, and how they know what they know. In this way, teachers begin to introduce children to the important scientific practice of using evidence to support claims. (This aspect of teaching is explored in greater depth in Chapter 4.)

Make Informed Decisions

Good teachers make informed decisions continually. They observe children so that they know what to do next. This includes asking questions to check for understanding, drawing children's attention to something they had not noticed, making comments that prompt children to think about something in a new way, posing problems for them to solve, or asking them to explain what they have done. Teachers intervene with questions, problems, and challenges in order to promote children's thinking. This important topic is addressed and elaborated on in much greater depth in later chapters.

Because good teachers understand that young children's thinking is not compartmentalized into tidy boxes labeled "Science," "Math," "Social Studies," "Reading," "Writing," and the like, they make decisions about how to integrate the curriculum across multiple content domains. Content from science is actually ideal for this sort of integration because it offers so many opportunities for children to count, measure, sort, classify, write, talk, and explain. Chapter 4 discusses the many ways that this can be done using R&P.

Good teachers also understand how important it is to document children's learning. They continually gather evidence that illustrates what and how children are thinking. They use this evidence to individualize their instruction, plan future experiences, and communicate with parents, administrators, and other stakeholders. Because of an increasing focus on standards, teachers are constantly asked to justify how they spend each minute in their classrooms. Documentation is a powerful tool for illustrating how literacy and mathematics standards are being met in an authentic context. Chapter 4 provides examples of documentation and describes how to actively involve children in the documentation process.

ADDRESSING STANDARDS IN RAMPS AND PATHWAYS

The field of science education, like all other fields of education today, has an abundance of standards. The standards that are most relevant to R&P are the recently released *Next Generation Science Standards* (NGSS; National Research Council, 2013). These standards interweave science and engineering in a manner that respects the integration of the four STEM disciplines.

Even though the NGSS are explicitly for grades K–12, they are also relevant to preschool. In fact, the state of Massachusetts has recently developed preschool standards that closely resemble the NGSS (Massachusetts Department of Education, 2013). In this chapter, I describe parts of the *Framework for K–12 Science Education* (see Figure 1.2) from the NGSS and illustrate how these standards can be found in national early childhood program standards, drawing from the *Head Start Child Development and Early Learning Framework* (CDELF; Office of Head Start, 2011) and the National Association for the Education of Young Children's *Early Childhood Program Standards and Accreditation Criteria* (ECPSAC; National Association for the Education of Young Children [NAEYC], 2014). Linking these early childhood standards demonstrates the alignment between the science education community and the early childhood community concerning how best to approach STEM in the early years. The NGSS as well as additional sets of standards are referenced and discussed in greater detail in Chapters 3, 7, and 8. A more complete list of the relevant standards addressed by R&P can be found on the R&P website (www.rampsandpathways.org). The ways in which Common Core State Standards (CCSS) align with R&P activities are discussed in great detail in subsequent chapters that elaborate more specifically on mathematical thinking and learning during R&P.

The NGSS (NRC, 2013) are organized into a framework that consists of Scientific and Engineering Practices (SEP), Crosscutting Concepts, and Disciplinary Core Ideas (see Figure 1.2). The Disciplinary Core Ideas are addressed in Chapter 3 concerning physical science content. Here, I discuss the Scientific and Engineering Practices and the Crosscutting Concepts, and demonstrate how they are included in the Head Start and NAEYC standards.

Scientific and Engineering Practices

In *Taking Science to School* (NRC, 2007), the authors argue that science education works best when it reflects the view that science is both a body of knowledge *and* a way of knowing the world, both content *and* process. This approach recognizes that children cannot ask a question, formulate a hypothesis, or design an experiment unless that question, hypothesis, or experiment is about *something*. So content and process are inseparable. The NGSS have addressed this by organizing the processes of scientific inquiry into eight Scientific and Engineering Practices (SEP; see the first column in Figure 1.2). Because these eight practices overlap somewhat, I discuss them together rather than separately.

R&P activities provide young children with rich, meaningful, and purposeful opportunities to engage in all of these practices, although some adults may not recognize when they do so. The first practice, *Asking questions (science) and defining problems (engineering)*, is fundamental

Figure 1.2. NGSS Framework for K–12 Science Education

Scientific and Engineering Practices	Crosscutting Concepts	Disciplinary Core Ideas	
• Asking questions (science) and defining problems (engineering)	• Patterns	**Physical Sciences**	**Life Sciences**
	• Cause and effect: Mechanism and explanation	PS1. Matter and interaction	LS 1. From molecules to organisms: Structures and processes
• Developing and using models		PS 2. Motion and stability: Forces and interactions	
• Planning and carrying out investigations			
• Analyzing and interpreting data	• Scale, proportion, and quantity	PS 3. Energy	LS 2. Ecosystems: Interactions, energy, and dynamics
• Using mathematics and computational thinking	• Systems and system models	PS 4. Waves and their applications in technology for information transfer	
	• Energy and matter		LS 3. Heredity: Inheritance and variation of traits
• Constructing explanations (science) and designing solutions (engineering)	• Structure and function	**Engineering, Technology, and the Applications of Science**	LS 4. Biological evolution: Unity and diversity
	• Stability and change	ETS 1. Engineering design	**Earth and Space Sciences**
• Engaging in argument from evidence			ESS 1. Earth's place in the universe
• Obtaining, evaluating, and communicating information		ETS 2. Links among engineering, technology, science, and society	ESS 2. Earth's systems
			ESS 3. Earth and human activity

Source: NRC, 2013.

to STEM and to R&P. By combining science and engineering, the NGSS acknowledge that these processes are in fact two sides of the same coin. All science and engineering learning experiences start with a question or a problem, and they all provide opportunities for the other seven practices, to varying degrees.

For example, children might pose the initial *question* (SEP #1) "Can I get this marble to move on this ramp without touching it?" and then *plan and carry out an investigation* (SEP #3) of how to get the marble to move. When they launch their marble and find it doesn't work the way they want, they must make observations (*obtaining, evaluating, and communicating information*; SEP #8) to figure out why it did not work. This process of making observations and organizing them mentally is an early example of *analyzing and interpreting data* (SEP #4).

Once children have figured out the need for an incline, another question they frequently ask concerns how fast different objects roll down ramps. They might decide to build side-by-side ramp structures and conduct races to see which objects roll fastest down a ramp. For this, they must figure out how to use the same number and size of blocks for each ramp in order to have ramps of identical heights (*using mathematics and computational thinking*; SEP #5). As they compare the speeds of different objects moving down the ramps, they use evidence to *construct explanations* (SEP #6) that answer their questions about which objects roll faster. In the process of building and playing with their ramp structures, they continually communicate with others (adults and peers) about what they have done, what worked, and what didn't work (*engaging in argument from evidence*; SEP #7; and *obtaining, evaluating and communicating information*; SEP #8).

The NGSS rightly pair asking questions with defining problems, because these two processes are so similar. From very simple problems (such as "How can I get a marble to move along the ramp without touching it or blowing on it?) to very complex problems with multiple components that must work together (such as designing a ramp structure that includes corners, jumps, hills, and drops), young children can be seen *defining problems* (SEP #1) and *designing solutions* (SEP #6). For example, once children have figured out that they need an incline to get a marble to move, they often decide to build long ramp structures (longer than the longest ramp segments). This leads to the problem of joining ramp segments. When their marble flies off the ramp at the place where two ramp segments come together, they must figure out why it is happening and how to prevent it (*designing solutions*; SEP #6). Through close observation and analysis (SEP #4 and #8), they begin to notice whenever the first ramp segment is placed underneath the second segment, the marble comes to a stop, but whenever the first segment is placed over the second segment, the marble continues to roll. With experience, they begin to learn how to visualize a ramp structure and how it will work without actually testing it (*developing and using models*; SEP #2).

The complexity of children's design challenges can be seen when children pose for themselves the problem of designing a ramp structure with a right-angle turn. After children figure out that a marble will move faster on a ramp with a steep incline, they commonly create structures with very steep inclines (perhaps they find the speed exciting). The problem comes when they first try to add a corner. They often simply place one ramp segment at a right angle to the first ramp, and are surprised when the marble continues in the same direction and goes off the ramp. After multiple observations of the marble not turning the corner, they begin to analyze their data (SEP #4). That is, they notice that every time the marble goes down the ramp, it rolls straight instead of turning. Children will often place a block at the corner to stop the marble. However, if the marble is traveling very fast (because of the steep incline), the marble either bounces off the block or knocks the block over. They may try this multiple times before they are convinced that it will not work.

Unlike adults, young children do not understand the rule that if you repeat an experiment the same way, under the same conditions, you will get roughly the same results. So they have to try it multiple times. But when they have collected enough data (it knocks down the block every time), they may decide that the problem is that the marble is traveling too fast. High speed is no longer viewed as something exciting and fun, but rather, is now considered an obstacle that prevents the marble from staying on the ramp.

In order to resolve their dilemma, children must ask the scientific question "What causes the marble to go faster or slower?" This further leads to a corresponding engineering design question: "How can I slow it down so it will turn the corner?" Children may try a different marble or release the marble at a different point on the ramp, but eventually, they arrive at the idea that they should change the incline. This involves thinking about the height of the support and the number of blocks they need to remove (or add) to change the incline (SEP #5).

Children test and retest their ideas, making changes to their design until they achieve success in getting the marble to turn the corner. Once children have achieved success, other children may ask them how they made the corner work. This question requires thoughtful reflection on the part of the designers, examining what they did, and explaining why they think it worked (*constructing explanations and designing solutions*; SEP #6).

The scientific and engineering practices are reflected in two domains of the CDELF: *Logic and Reasoning* and *Science Knowledge and Skills* (see Figure 1.3, center column). With regard to science, the Head Start standards call for children to develop "the skills to observe and collect information and use it to ask questions, predict, explain, and draw conclusions" (Office of Head Start, 2011, p. 18); all of these are skills addressed in the NGSS.

Engineering and problem solving are also addressed in the CDELF. As children pose more and more elaborate design problems within their ramp structures, they inevitably encounter problems that cause their system to fail. The Head Start CDELF standards call for children to "recognize, understand, and analyze a problem and draw on knowledge or experience to seek solutions to a problem" (Office of Head Start, 2011, p. 12). Children's efforts to locate the source of a problem and make adjustments provide them with rich opportunities to engage in the NGSS Scientific and Engineering Practices. It is clear that these practices are recognized and valued by Head Start.

Teachers play an important role throughout scientific investigation and engineering design processes. Teachers carefully observe children's progress over time. When a child has solved a problem, the teacher prompts the child to explain what he or she did and how it worked. The ECPSAC address the teacher's role in supporting the process of doing science most directly in Standard 2 (the Curriculum Standard) (see Figure 1.3, right column). Standard 2.A.08 states that the materials and equipment provided for children should "encourage exploration, experimentation, and discovery" (NAEYC, 2014, p. 10). Again, these are addressed in the NGSS practices, although the NGSS are much more specific.

Standard 2 also calls for teachers to provide opportunities for children to engage in these practices. Under the content area for science (Standard 2.G.), the criteria state that children should be provided with opportunities and materials "that encourage them to use the five senses to observe, explore, and experiment with scientific phenomena" (2.G.03); "to collect data and to represent and document their findings" (2.G.05); "that encourage them to think, question, and reason about observed and inferred phenomena" (2.G.06); and "that encourage them to discuss scientific concepts in everyday conversation" (2.G.07). It is clear that the scientific and engineering practices identified in the NGSS are recognized and valued by NAEYC (see Figure 1.3).

The more adults understand that STEM experiences such as R&P afford young children rich opportunities to engage in the practices of STEM, the more likely learning and developmental outcomes will be maximized.

Crosscutting Concepts

For decades, voices in the education community have criticized education at all levels for being "a mile wide and an inch deep." As seen in the foreword to *Taking Science to School*, "the current organization of science curriculum and instruction does not provide the kind of support for science learning that results in *deep understanding of scientific ideas*" (italics added; NRC, 2007, p. viii).

Figure 1.3. Aligning NGSS Scientific and Engineering Practices and Crosscutting Concepts with Head Start and NAEYC Standards

Next Generation Science Standards (NGSS)	Head Start CDELF Domains	NAEYC Accreditation Standards and Criteria
Scientific and Engineering Practices	*Logic and Reasoning*	*Standard 2A: Curriculum—Essential Characteristics*
1. Asking questions (science) and defining problems (engineering)	Reasoning and problem solving: The ability to recognize, understand, and analyze a problem and draw on knowledge or experience to seek solutions to a problem	Materials and equipment encourage exploration, experimentation, and discovery.
2. Developing and using models		*Standard 2G: Curriculum—Curriculum Content Area for Cognitive Development: Science*
3. Planning and carrying out investigations	*Science Knowledge and Skills*	2.G.02 Children are provided varied opportunities and materials to learn key content and principles of science such as structure and property of matter.
4. Analyzing and interpreting data	Scientific skills and method: The skills to observe and collect information and use it to ask questions, predict, explain, and draw conclusions	2.G.03 Children are provided varied opportunities and materials that encourage them to use the five senses to observe, explore, and experiment with scientific phenomena.
5. Using mathematics and computational thinking		
6. Constructing explanations (science) and designing solutions (engineering)	*Mathematics Knowledge and Skills*	2.G.05 Children are provided varied opportunities and materials to collect data and to represent and document their findings.
7. Engaging in argument from evidence	Patterns: The recognition of patterns, sequencing, and critical thinking skills necessary to predict and classify objects in a pattern	2.G.06 Children are provided varied opportunities and materials that encourage them to think, question, and reason about observed and inferred phenomena.
8. Obtaining, evaluating and communicating information		2.G.07 Children are provided varied opportunities and materials that encourage them to discuss scientific concepts in everyday conversation.
Crosscutting Concepts	*Science Knowledge and Skills*	*Standard 2F: Curriculum—Curriculum Content Area for Cognitive Development: Early Mathematics*
1. Patterns	Scientific skills and method: Conceptual knowledge of the natural and physical world (observes, describes, and discusses properties of materials and transformation of substances)	2.F.07 Children are provided varied opportunities and materials that help them recognize and name repeating patterns.
2. Cause and effect: Mechanism and explanation		
3. Scale, proportion, and quantity		
4. Systems and system models		
5. Energy and matter		
6. Structure and function		
7. Stability and change		

The NGSS respond to this challenge with their inclusion of Crosscutting Concepts that are applied across all areas of STEM and at every grade level (see Figure 1.2). These concepts provide a unifying structure that will help deepen K–12 students' understanding of science and engineering. The ECPSAC include many of these concepts, and recognize the importance of talking about scientific concepts in Standard 2.G.07: "Children are provided varied opportunities and materials that encourage them to discuss scientific concepts in everyday conversation" (NAEYC, 2014, p. 19). Some of the Crosscutting Concepts (such as patterns) are familiar to early educators, while others may be somewhat new. Because some early educators may not be familiar with these concepts, they are described below.

Patterns. Instruction in how to continue simple repeating patterns shows up frequently in typical early childhood classrooms, justified as part of early childhood mathematics curricula. It appears in the CDELF in the section on mathematics and in the ECPSAC Standard 2.F. 08 (the section of the curriculum content area focused on mathematics): "Children are provided varied opportunities and materials that help them recognize and name repeating patterns" (NAEYC, 2014, p. 17). It likewise informs ECPSAC Standard 2.F.10: "Kindergartners are provided varied experiences and materials to create, represent, discuss, and extend repeating and growing patterns" (NAEYC, 2014, p. 18).

On the other hand, early childhood teachers are less likely to draw children's attention to patterns that can be observed in everyday life. In actuality, children's natural (and human-made) surroundings are filled with patterns, such as the changes in a tree's shadow over the course of a day, from long to short and then back to long (earth science); plants with specific leaf clusters (life science); or the predictable green, yellow, and red sequence of traffic lights (technology).

In the case of R&P, children often use patterns in the design of their ramp structures. As in the case of the examples previously mentioned, some children may not readily recognize the patterns they create without adults drawing attention to them. Others pick up on successful patterns in designs and replicate them in subsequent ramp structures.

Cause and effect. Cause-and-effect relationships are also familiar to most early educators. Some causal relationships are easier to draw children's attention to than others, for various reasons. Children might have difficulty figuring out why a plant died, although they may have many ideas (too much water, too little water, too little sunlight, too cold, and so on). However, experiences with physical science and engineering provide myriad opportunities to engage in causal reasoning.

Children can figure out many causal relationships using R&P materials. For example, children can change the speed of the marble by raising and lowering the incline. With experience, they can determine that if they want to knock down a block at the end of a ramp, a large, heavy marble works better than a small, lighter marble. Children also learn that marbles can travel down one ramp and up another one, but they can't go over a hill that is taller than the original release point of the marble.

Energy and matter. Experiences such as these allow children to have direct experiences with another crosscutting concept—energy and matter. When children compare what happens when they release heavier and lighter marbles, they construct a practical understanding about different marbles' weight (or mass) in relation to energy. Heavier marbles have more kinetic energy at the bottom of the ramp than lighter marbles. Teachers would not necessarily use this terminology, but they could discuss with young children what they observe about the differences between the heavier and lighter marbles, and encourage children to use language to describe the differences.

Scale, proportion, and quantity. The concepts of scale, proportion, and quantity can be challenging for young children to use and understand, but children can begin to reason about and notice aspects of these concepts during R&P activities. For example, children can release a marble at different points on a ramp and observe that the distance the marble rolls across the floor is in direct proportion to the release point.

Systems. Ramps provide an excellent introduction to the concept of systems because a ramp structure is a system in which all the parts interact, and changes to one part of the system result in changes to other parts. A good example of this can be seen when young children first start to link multiple ramp segments together to make a longer ramp. Sometimes they will shift one end of a ramp segment left or right, not realizing that when they do so, the other end of the segment shifts in the opposite direction. This is an early (and meaningful) introduction to the concept of systems using R&P materials.

Structure and function. Structure and function may be overlooked by teachers and perhaps less emphasized as a result. However, the idea that the characteristics of an object and the materials it is made of can influence the way it functions is fairly simple for young children to understand. For example, some metals (like iron) are hard and are used to create hand tools such as hammers. A wooden hammer does not function the same way as a metal hammer. A wooden hammer can drive some objects into a substance (such as pounding golf tees into a pumpkin), but for other tasks, such as hammering a nail into a block of wood, it is not effective. Learning about the properties of materials is included in the ECPSAC Standard 2.G.02 (NAEYC, 2014) and in the CDELF (Office of Head Start, 2011).

When children build with blocks, they deal directly with structure and function. Children quickly learn that wooden blocks provide a more stable foundation for a ramp than cardboard or foam blocks, that large blocks provide a more stable foundation than small blocks, and that the orientation of the block (placed on the largest surface) makes a difference in stabilizing a structure.

Stability and change. The final crosscutting concept in the NGSS is stability and change. Everything in the world, both natural and human-made, can be described in terms of stability and change. Children experience changes in their own bodies (e.g., they grow too large for their clothes and shoes, they lose teeth, and so forth). These kinds of life changes provide an excellent introduction to one of the characteristics of living things: Living organisms change (although some organisms change faster than others, and some changes are so slight as to be imperceptible except over long expanses of time).

On the other hand, individual blocks and ramps are fairly constant, static, and stable. Once placed on the floor, blocks do not tend to move unless some outside force acts on them. Similarly, if children want to change the motion of a marble on a ramp, they must initiate the change themselves. Children will rearrange (redesign) their ramp structure in some way (raising or lowering the height of the ramp, adding or subtracting ramp segments, and so on).

CONCLUSION

The R&P team's experience has been that children find building and using ramp structures highly enjoyable: They return to them again and again, they play with them for long periods of time, and they display positive emotions while they are engaged with them (such as smiles, laughter, animated discussion, and excitement). This enjoyment could easily lead to the development of positive attitudes about STEM that will contribute to children's later school success in STEM. It may even lead some children to make career choices in STEM fields. Finally, children often devote a great deal of time and effort to refining the designs of their ramp structures, and are often justifiably proud of their creations. When children construct ramp structures that work the way they want them to work, this sends a message to children that they are capable problem-solvers. At the very least, enjoyable experiences such as these can be expected to lead children to view school—and specifically STEM—in a positive light.

CHAPTER 2

Implementing Ramps and Pathways in the Classroom

Rosemary Geiken, Jill Uhlenberg, and Sonia Yoshizawa

After seeing the value of Ramps and Pathways (R&P), many teachers want to jump right in. At workshops we hear teachers say they want to get ramps right away and take them to the classroom! Though we applaud these teachers' enthusiasm, we recommend that teachers take some time to plan and prepare before introducing ramp materials into the classroom. In this chapter, we share with you what we have learned about preparing the environment for R&P, introducing ramps for the first time, and engaging learners in thinking about their work with R&P.

PREPARING THE ENVIRONMENT FOR R&P

The classroom environment sends powerful messages to children about what can and cannot go on in the room, how people relate to one another, and how learning will take place (Dodge, Colker, & Heroman, 2002). Creating a supportive environment that lets children know it is safe to successfully try out ideas, even if they fail, while engaging with ramps requires thoughtful preparation by the classroom teacher.

During development of R&P, we worked closely with teachers who were piloting R&P in their classrooms. Over the course of a year we went into their classrooms, observed children engaging with ramps, listened to teachers explain what worked and what was challenging, and learned about the importance of the classroom environment in supporting children's scientific thinking. In this section, we focus on what the pilot teachers taught us about environments that worked. We share our learning on three key aspects of a supportive environment: (1) a physical environment that contains interesting materials to manipulate, (2) an intellectual environment that allows time for children to develop and try out ideas with those materials, and (3) a social environment that conveys the message that communication is a valuable part of learning (Wilson, n.d.). In reality, the three aspects combine to be a powerful influence, but for the sake of discussion, we separate them in the next section.

**THREE KEY ASPECTS OF A SUPPORTIVE
ENVIRONMENT WHEN CONSIDERING R&P**

1. *Physical Environment*
   a. *Materials:* Provide interesting materials for children to
      manipulate.
   b. *Space:* Be flexible with space to allow children to explore with
      ramps indoors and outdoors.
2. *Intellectual Environment:* Allow time for children to develop and
   try out their ideas with the materials.
3. *Social Environment:* Collaboration and communication are
   valuable parts of learning and are characteristics of
   mathematicians and scientists.

The Physical Environment

The physical environment has the capacity to invite children's attention
to and involvement with materials (Gestwicki, 2007). With regard to the
Inquiry Teaching Model (ITM), the physical environment has the power
to support or squelch opportunities for children's exploration, problem
solving, investigation, and communication. As we worked with teachers in
planning the physical environment to provide maximum opportunity for
children to engage in inquiry with R&P, we considered materials, accessibil-
ity and storage of materials, and space for ramps construction.

   Materials. Materials offered to children should provide interesting challenges for all ages, developmental levels, and abilities, and inspire children
to experiment in many different ways. Some suppliers of commercial materials have developed soft plastic cup-shaped hosing. We find these frustrating
for children because they move too easily from the desired position. They
also remove opportunity for children to problem-solve how to turn corners.
We found cove molding, 1¾-inch wide and flat on the bottom, to be most
effective for R&P. Narrower widths do not accommodate a variety of sizes
of marbles, or other objects. Wider widths cause marbles to "wobble" too
much while rolling down. Cove molding can be purchased at most building
supply stores (EverTrue 1¾-inch Stain Grade Radiata Pine, sold in 8-foot
lengths) and can be cut into desired lengths. We have used 1-, 2-, 3-, and
4-foot lengths, although any lengths will work (see Photo 2.1).
   Most classrooms of 16–18 children need at least 12 segments of each
length for all children to build and be able to move beyond simple structures. Some building supply stores will cut the cove molding for you. Another option would be to cut your own. If you choose to create your

Photo 2.1. Cove Molding Cut Into Four Different Lengths for Building Ramp Structures

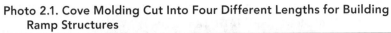

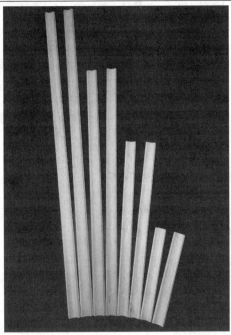

own classroom set, be sure to sand the ends so there are no rough edges. Teachers have often involved parents in helping with cutting and sanding or have had local service organizations do it as part of their community project work.

One preschool teacher chose an innovative approach to prepare her ramps. She organized cutting and sanding as a learning opportunity and a classroom community project for her children. She had children measure and mark the lengths needed for ramp sections. They then sawed the molding into the desired lengths and sanded the ends. Having children involved in this way not only piqued their interest in ramps, but it was a rich opportunity to learn about measurement!

In addition to ramp sections, children will need items that can travel along the ramps. Marbles of different sizes move easily down cove molding ramps. In classrooms with children who mouth objects (usually younger than 3 years), marbles need to be tested to ensure they do not fit through the choke tube (a minimum of 35 millimeters in diameter). Older children can use a variety of sizes, giving them the opportunity to compare the movement of large and small marbles along ramp sections. Other variations include steel marbles (allowing the opportunity to observe how differences in mass lead to differences in the ways objects move), blocks or other objects that

CHILDREN USE MATH SKILLS AS THEY HELP PREPARE FOR RAMPS AND PATHWAYS

Having children measure and cut the ramp sections allows children to meet the following National Council for Teachers of Mathematics Standards for pre-K–2: Measurement:

- Recognize the attributes of length, volume, weight, area, and time
- Compare and order objects according to these attributes
- Understand how to measure using nonstandard and standard units

This activity also presents an opportunity to meet the following Common Core State Standards:

- CCSS.Math.Content.1.MD.A.1: Order three objects by length: compare the lengths of two objects indirectly by using a third object.
- CCSS.Math.Content.1.MD.A.2: Express the length of an object as a whole number of length units, by laying multiple copies of a shorter object (the length unit) end to end; understand that the length measurement of an object is the number of same-size length units that span it with no gaps or overlaps.
- CCSS.Math.Content.2.MD.A.1: Measure the length of an object by selecting and using appropriate tools such as rulers, yardsticks, meter sticks, and measure tapes.

will not roll, and items that roll differently (such as spools, egg-shaped objects, spheres with bumps, and so on).

Some children may discover that miniature toy cars roll on ramps. However, these cars do not move as well as marbles, and differences in how they roll are not readily explainable. Also, some children focus more on pretend play with cars, particularly Matchbox cars. If the teacher's agenda is scientific play or exploration, we suggest the removal of cars after some initial investigation.

As children explore ramp materials, they need a way to prop up ramp sections. Often, children use whatever is available, such as shelves, chairs, and tables. Children also use wooden unit blocks, large interlocking blocks, or large cardboard blocks. Some teachers brought in cardboard boxes (with holes cut in the sides as shown in Photo 2.2) to be used for propping up ramp sections.

Photo 2.2. Children Prop Ramp Sections Using Cardboard Boxes

By far the best materials to use with ramps are wooden unit blocks. Teachers with whom we have worked on R&P report that unit blocks are extremely important to the success of R&P. As one 2nd-grade teacher stated,

> Blocks are more important than you would ever believe. We started out with Kleenex boxes and egg crates and stuff, but once the children got blocks they were doing more jumps and corners. They were doing so much more with the blocks! (2nd-grade teacher, personal communication, April 2008)

The unit blocks serve as much more than supports. Unit blocks provide a standard measure so children have control over how much they vary the height of the ramp and are able to compare the height of two different ramps. As children build more complex structures, unit blocks are essential for carrying out their plans (such as making a marble turn a corner, creating a ramp structure with both downhill and uphill ramps, and so forth). We encourage teachers implementing R&P to make unit blocks available, stored near the ramps.

When considering how to store materials, it is important that children are able to reach materials easily on their own. We have found that a large

BENEFITS OF UNIT BLOCKS

There are many benefits to having unit blocks available for children to use in building structures. The following list illustrates just a few of these benefits:

Space: determining what size and how many blocks are needed to fill a space to support a ramp

Numbers: counting blocks needed to support a ramp at the desired height

One-to-one correspondence: working to make two ramps the same height and figuring out that there must be the same number of blocks for each ramp

Balance: discovering that blocks are more stable when set flat rather than on end

Spatial visualization: figuring out where to place blocks to make a marble turn a corner

Spatial orientation: rotating and changing position of blocks in the ramp structure

plastic clothes hamper on wheels, propped up against a wall for support, holds all the ramp sections and can easily be rolled out for use. For younger children, the hamper can be placed on the floor horizontally so ramp sections can be more easily removed. Other teachers have used tall metal wastebaskets, golf bags, or large containers for holding giftwrap.

You may find other containers for storing ramps but we caution you to try them out before presenting them to young children. Get down on your knees so you are at a child's height and try to lift various ramp sections out of the container. You will want to make sure that a young child can easily remove the longest sections without tipping over the container and possibly causing injury.

Marbles and other objects for rolling down ramp sections can be stored in a divided organizer, often found in hobby stores or discount stores. You may also use fishing lure storage containers found in the sporting goods sections of discount stores. The compartments in these organizers can be used to house various size marbles. Many of these organizers also have a large open area for storing other objects.

If unit blocks are an essential part of your classroom, your blocks are most likely stored and organized on shelves according to your individual classroom needs. Based on our experience with using blocks as part of R&P, we have some suggestions for storing blocks in a way that will enhance children's learning. Beth Van Meeteren, director of Regents' Center at the University of Northern Iowa, is researching engineering processes with young children. She has worked in the classroom and has extensive experience with ramps and unit blocks. Beth recommends storing blocks on the shelf so that all similar blocks are in one area. In addition, when placing the blocks on the shelf, arrange blocks so children can easily see the angles (see Photo 2.3).

Arranging blocks in this way encourages children to think about the properties of the blocks before taking them off the shelves.

As you plan the physical environment for R&P materials, keep in mind that how and where you store materials will suggest what can be done. Storing ramp sections in the block area will invite children to use blocks as part of their ramp construction. Keeping materials visible at all times sends the message to children that you believe these materials are a worthwhile and vital part of the classroom.

Space. Space is an issue in many classrooms. Once children start to build ramp structures, they want to build bigger and bigger ramps! Often, this means longer ramps, and it is not unusual to walk into a classroom where R&P is being implemented and see a long line of ramp sections propped up on every chair and desk in the room. But not every classroom has the luxury of that kind of space. As we observed different classrooms during our pilot project, we found that children were very creative in using small spaces and were still able to experiment with the materials. In one classroom, children built ramp structures that went around the perimeter of the classroom. They arranged ramp sections to go behind file cabinets, along whiteboard and window ledges, and under tables.

Photo 2.3. Store Blocks to Show Angles

When adequate space is not available in the classroom, teachers often find other solutions. Some teachers in the pilot project offered only shorter ramp sections to minimize the space needed for ramp construction. This solution was a good way to introduce ramps, but children soon needed more space. Teachers then found space in hallways, lunchrooms, open conference rooms, or outside. One group of kindergarten children took ramps outside when classroom space limited the length of ramps they could build. Once outside, children used playground equipment and tree stumps as supports and built long, elaborate structures with hills and corners. Moving ramps to other locations also allowed children to observe how marbles rolled differently on different surfaces (tile, wood, carpet, grass, and so forth).

Intellectual Environment

The physical aspect of the environment involves thoughtful use of materials and space to provide children the opportunity to engage in inquiry. Careful preparation of the physical environment is necessary but not sufficient to promote high levels of reasoning. In this section, we talk about the intellectual environment necessary for children to think about and reflect on their actions with materials as they explore, problem-solve, investigate, and communicate. Teachers who support children's thinking create an intellectual environment in which it is safe for children to try out their ideas, observe what happens, and then try again with new information in mind. This type of environment is created when teachers think of activities in terms of possibilities for learning and establish schedules that allow children ample time to engage in ramp activities.

Possibilities for learning. In Chapter 1, we discussed the importance of knowing about children's ideas and where they come from in order to provide appropriate experiences and to support children's learning. One way to figure out where children's ideas come from is to play with and explore ramps before putting them out for children. This is critical for teachers in preparing the intellectual environment. Exploration is so important to R&P that we devote large blocks of time during our workshops for teachers to play with the materials and see what they can do. Our experiences have shown us that adults are uniformly intrigued by ramps, and we observe many of the same actions as we see with children. We see the same surprise when things don't work as expected. Surprise (evidence of what Piaget calls disequilibrium) can be a very valuable experience because this is what children experience all the time. When adults experience that same surprise and then revise their actions, they begin to make some of the same connections children make.

You do not have to attend a workshop to experience this. You can find other teachers in your program who are interested and together you can explore ramps. If there are no other teachers to work with, do not let that stop you. Although we believe it is more beneficial to work with others and discuss your thinking, you can do it alone. Get out the materials and see what you can do. How can you make the marble move without touching it? Can you make a marble travel up a ramp section? Think about your thinking as you work with the materials. What are the possibilities in this activity for children? What can they learn? What connections can they make as they observe ramps in action? As you investigate, take notes of what you have figured out. These notes will help you when you observe children and plan your interventions.

Some of the most powerful learning in R&P consists of connections that are made between actions on the materials and reactions of the objects. For example, if four unit blocks are placed under the high end of the ramp, the marble travels faster than if there are two unit blocks under the high end. This offers the possibility for the child to construct a relationship between the height of the ramp and the speed of the marble. As you work with the materials, you will identify numerous connections or relationships that children will have the possibility to construct: size of the marble and how far it rolls, shape of the object and how it moves (or does not move) on the ramp, and many more (see Appendix 2.1). Connections you identify can be used to plan lessons and can be aligned with standards to document the learning that is taking place (see Appendix 2.2).

Scheduling for ramps. Children's inquiry is supported by a schedule that allows ample time for children to engage with the materials. Materials must be available to children for a sufficient length of time that allows for extended exploration, investigation, and experimentation. Here, we refer to time both in terms of minutes in a day and in terms of days, weeks, months, and even years.

Children's opportunity to choose is as important as ensuring that children have ample time to work with R&P. This goes back to the vital role of interest in children's engagement and reasoning. Children who choose to work with ramps are interested in trying out their ideas, and as a result, they think deeply about their work. Children who are assigned to ramps may engage to please the teacher rather than investigate to figure something out. In some classrooms, it may occasionally be necessary to assign children to go to the ramps center. Some children never choose to go to the ramps center. In that case, it may be necessary to assign them to the ramps center to explore the materials. In many cases, this initial exploration captures their interest and keeps them engaged.

Daily schedule. With regard to time within the daily schedule, we have found that children need extended periods of time to engage fully with the materials. Ideally, a 45-minute block per day is the minimum needed for children to be able to engage deeply in investigations. This is not to say that all children will engage with ramps for 45 minutes at a time, or that children should be *required* to engage for any specified length of time. What we are saying is that we have routinely observed even preschool-age children engage for 45 minutes or longer, and they have been highly productive for the entire duration. We have also found that when children are given too little time, they seem to be less engaged in the activities, their ramp structures are not as complex, and their investigations do not go as far as when they are allowed more time.

It is important for teachers not only to allow for ample uninterrupted time for exploration with R&P materials but also to recognize when children need more time. We all have experienced how frustrating it can be when we are on a roll in working to accomplish a goal and may not be ready to quit when time runs short. One preschool teacher commented on how she handles this with the children in her class: "I usually know which students are on the verge of a breakthrough and allow them to continue with ramps." This teacher understands that the daily schedule can be altered slightly to allow more time so that the children in her class can feel the sense of accomplishment that comes with achieving a goal or figuring out something new.

Teachers with whom we have worked on R&P found ways to set their schedules so children are allowed choice and have uninterrupted time to work. During the pilot phase of our R&P project, we asked participating teachers how they dealt with scheduling issues to allow ample time for R&P. One kindergarten teacher reported, "It fit in very easily. The activities can be *totally* student-directed. My students are motivated to go back and try new things day after day." By providing ample time for her students to direct their activity with ramps, the teacher was able to work with other children during that time and do a quick check of the ramp builders in between her work with others.

In 1st- and 2nd-grade classrooms, some teachers offered R&P as one choice during small-group time. The teacher worked with one group of students, one group was involved in extension activities related to the small-group lesson, and one group had the opportunity to engage in R&P (see Photo 2.4).

In between small groups, the teacher visited the R&P activity to observe children's work and facilitate as needed (see Chapter 4 for an expanded discussion of this schedule).

Even teachers who have different groups of children for separate morning and afternoon sessions can provide adequate time for these activities. Below is a sample daily schedule to illustrate that a 45-minute block can be fit into a 2.5-hour preschool class.

8:30 Quiet activities (puzzles, books, and so on)
8:45–9:05 Group time
9:05–9:50 Centers (includes a ramp center)

9:50–10:00 Cleanup
10:00–10:30 Wash hands, snack, brush teeth
10:30–10:45 Gross motor
10:45–11:00 Storytime, prepare for home

Though we do believe that a minimum 45-minute block of time is ideal, we also realize that teachers face challenges in schedules that may not allow this. Our hope is that you do not abandon ramps because you cannot find this block of time, but instead that you will start small and once you see the benefits, you will find creative ways to increase the amount of time available. At the beginning of the pilot project, the majority of teachers reported having concerns about finding time. By the end, they had found ways to offer children the time needed for the rich learning that takes place with R&P.

Long-term scheduling. It is most beneficial to make R&P materials available to children every day, year-round. This can easily be done by keeping ramps in the block center. In most early childhood classrooms, the block center is a permanent part of the classroom, and only accessories are rotated. By making ramps a permanent part of the block center, teachers allow children opportunities to revisit their ideas, make changes and adaptations,

Photo 2.4. Students Work with Ramps While Teacher Conducts Small-Group Instruction

and add new layers of complexity to their structures. Some teachers who have sufficient space allow children to leave their ramp structures up for days, as long as children are continuing to work on them. Our experience has been that children do not tire of using ramps. Interest may wax and wane somewhat, but in general, building ramp structures remains a favorite activity throughout the year.

In classrooms without a block center, R&P materials should be placed in an area that is easily accessible to children and allows for room to build. When this area is a shared area and is needed for other classroom activities, children often have to stop work before they are finished with their structures. When this occurs, it is respectful to document the child's work and save it so the child can revisit it the next day. Documentation can be a digital photo or a child's drawing. We have been surprised by children's ability to draw their structures, look at the picture a day later (or even longer), and reconstruct their work.

We have also found that interest in ramps will continue across several years. At the Freeburg Early Childhood Program, where the R&P activities were developed, children had experiences with ramps from the time they entered preschool as 3-year-olds until they left the school at the end of 2nd grade. These children exhibited remarkable knowledge and skills in building ramp structures. Photos of their structures can be seen throughout this book.

Social Environment

Inquiry science experiences such as those of R&P occur best in a social environment of cooperation and collaboration. The myth of the lonely scientist, working in isolation in his or her laboratory, is just that: a myth. In their research, Siry, Ziegler, and Max (2012) found that children co-construct science concepts through social interaction. Although experimenting and making errors, vital to the process of scientific inquiry, thrives best in an environment in which children are free to collaborate and take risks, most science curricula do not devote attention to this important aspect of instruction. In this section, we present some ways to support interaction and cooperation in the classroom.

Cooperation. The teacher–child relationship is at the center of any curriculum promoting inquiry. In traditional classrooms where the teacher is viewed as the authority, students' opportunities for cooperation are rare. Piaget (1965) calls this *heteronomous* and points out that children in this type of classroom do not feel the need to think for themselves or communicate their ideas to others. They learn to follow directions out of blind obedience and/or fear of punishment. They seldom act out of a sense of intellectual curiosity. They learn how to parrot correct answers, and if they are not sure of answers, they learn to remain silent. In other words, they take few risks. However, if children are to develop problem-solving abilities and truly engage in inquiry, teachers need to foster children's intellectual autonomy. The route to intellectual autonomy starts at cooperation. Two types of cooperation—cooperation between adults and children and cooperation among children—are important to inquiry science.

Cooperation between adults and children. Often, when adults refer to children as *cooperative* what they really mean is *compliant*. A more accurate way to think about cooperation is as *co-operation,* meaning two or more individuals operating together in a collaborative fashion. In a cooperative teacher–child relationship, the teacher considers the child's point of view and helps the child consider different points of view (DeVries & Zan, 1994, 2012). When this type of relationship exists, the teacher "asks rather than tells" and "suggests rather than demands" (DeVries & Zan, 1994, p. 50). When teachers create a social environment based on cooperation, they try to understand children's reasoning and facilitate the construction of knowledge. This is often easier said than done in working with young children, particularly when teachers watch a child struggling with a problem encountered while working with the ramps. By nature, early childhood teachers want to step in and help the child by fixing the problem or pointing out that what is being tried will not work.

In one kindergarten classroom, a teacher stood by and watched as a child tried to build a tower of blocks that could be used as a support for a ramp structure. The child made several attempts, always setting the unit block on end and adding more blocks on top. About the time the third block was added, the tower tumbled. Yet the child persisted. During this activity, the teacher intervened sparingly. When she noticed the child showing signs of frustration, the teacher pointed out that it was hard work to make a tower and asked what the child was trying to do. The child explained the goal of getting the blocks tall enough to support the ramp so it would go across two tables. When the blocks fell several more times, the teacher asked the child if there was a problem and asked the child to tell her about it. The child explained that the blocks were too wobbly and they kept falling. The teacher agreed and asked if there was something else the child could do to make the blocks less wobbly. The child looked at the fallen unit blocks and, on the next attempt, laid the unit block horizontally on the floor, providing a more stable foundation, and then continued to add more blocks horizontally until the tower reached the level needed to support the ramp.

In this example, the teacher asked questions to help her understand the child's reasoning and also helped the child facilitate construction of knowledge. Had the teacher stepped in and told the child how to build a more stable foundation, she would have sent the message that the child was not capable of solving problems. The child would probably have followed the teacher's direction but would not have constructed the connection between the placement of the blocks and the stability of the tower. This teacher valued the cooperative relationship and respected the child, but she admits she had to bite her tongue to avoid helping by giving the child direction! We will talk in later chapters about types of interventions to use with children to promote this type of cooperative relationship.

Cooperation among children. When children cooperate, they have the opportunity to think about how another person is thinking and feeling and take those thoughts and feelings into account. For example, when children cooperate in building a ramp structure, they must coordinate what each wants to do and come to some agreement. At times, children attempt to build large structures that require cooperation with peers. The children are so invested in their goal that they negotiate with others in order to be successful. This negotiation requires give-and-take as the children compromise on details of the design and learn to look at things from many perspectives. There are also times when children set aside conflict in order to cooperate in the building of a ramp structure.

An example of this occurred with three young children who were attempting to build a long ramp with four of the 4-foot sections of ramps. They wanted the beginning of the ramp to be on an incline but were having trouble lining up the sections. In the process, one of the children accidentally bumped the ramps, causing the structure to fall apart. Young children often do not differentiate action from intention (DeVries & Zan, 1994). In this case, the two remaining children accused the first child of purposely knocking the structure over and banned him from the activity. Later, after trying for several minutes, the two children realized they needed the third child to help hold things in place. They invited him back into the activity and he (reluctantly at first) joined in. It wasn't long before all three were again engaged in rich conversation as they figured out how to build their structure. It was clear that the original conflict was set aside as the children shared ideas and often compromised in order to build the long structure. Their squeals of joy when they succeeded were a celebration of a shared goal and repaired relationships.

Conflict resolution. Having a classroom with a social environment of mutual respect and cooperation does not mean being free of conflict. In fact, conflicts similar to those in the example above are quite common as children work through their ideas, learn to take others' perspectives, and interpret one another's actions. Teachers in the pilot project and in our workshops have concerns about conflict as they begin to implement ramps. Teachers are concerned that children will argue over materials, misuse materials, or have problems when structures get knocked over. Although we have rarely observed or heard of children misusing the materials, we know that conflict will occur. How the teacher views the conflict makes a difference.

If conflict is viewed as misbehavior, the teacher often takes over and stops it, never allowing the children to come to a resolution. When the issue is not resolved, the children continue to harbor negative feelings toward one another and the underlying problem is never addressed. If the teacher views the conflict as a lack of understanding of perspectives and not as misbehavior, the teacher will promote discussion that facilitates children's ability to see the issue from other perspectives. This allows them to work toward a resolution so the children can move forward. For a full discussion of how to handle conflict in the classroom, see DeVries and Zan (1994).

The Environment and the Inquiry Teaching Model

The previous section focused on the environment needed to maximize the learning that takes place during R&P activities. We address this first because thoughtful preparation of the environment needs to occur before introducing ramps to children. The availability of materials, use of space, allotment of time, and the atmosphere that encourages and supports risk-taking are equally critical to providing opportunities for inquiry (please refer to the ITM, Figure 1.1). The teacher will facilitate exploration, support problem solving, scaffold experimentation, and foster communication. In the remainder of this chapter, we present ways to introduce these opportunities to children as you get started with R&P.

INTRODUCING RAMPS TO CHILDREN

Engaging the learner is a key component of the ITM. When introducing ramps for the first time, you want to engage children by stimulating their interests and capitalizing on their natural curiosity. You can introduce ramps to the whole class at group time, or you may decide to place the materials in the ramp center and let children discover them during activity time.

Group Time

One preschool teacher, when introducing ramps, piqued 3-year-old children's interest by posing a problem and letting children suggest ways to solve it. The teacher set a 2-foot ramp section on the floor and placed a large marble in the middle of the ramp section. She asked the children, "How might we get this marble to move along the ramp?" Children brainstormed ways to get the marble to move and the teacher invited them to demonstrate their ideas. When many children started to have ideas, the teacher told the class that the materials would be available in the ramp center for them to use during activity time. This short activity stimulated children's interest in getting the marble to move along the ramp section and sparked their curiosity. They all wanted to try out their idea! Once at the ramp center, children tried out their ideas and in the process they found new problems to solve, which kept them engaged for a long time.

As noted in the ITM, one aspect of engaging learners is to identify the interests, prior ideas, skills, and experiences of the children in your group. In the scenario above, the teacher offered only one ramp section and posed a basic problem that she knew the children could easily solve. You will need to determine which materials to use and what problem to suggest when introducing ramps to your particular group of children, taking into account their prior experiences and skills. We recommend limiting the materials for this introduction so children can more easily generate ideas. Young children tend to focus on only one aspect of a situation and have difficulty if there are too many possibilities. If there are too many materials, the children may have trouble focusing.

When introducing ramps during group time, it is important to honor all responses, even ones that may not seem logical from an adult perspective. When children are invited to demonstrate their ideas, they have the opportunity to observe the reactions of objects and can then revise their original idea. If they are told their idea will not work, they may decide that their ideas are not worthy and may stop thinking about the problem. In other words, they lose interest and will not engage in inquiry.

After group time, place ramp materials in the ramp center and let children continue to try out their ideas. You may want to keep materials limited at first, but children will soon need to have more materials. Add these as you observe and see that children are ready for more challenges (see Chapter 4 for a more complete discussion of when to add materials).

Tabletop Ramps

Another teacher started R&P by introducing tabletop ramps. She provided only the 1-foot sections, some sponges, and a few marbles. She limited the space and avoided the frustration of having to chase marbles around the room by creating a board to be placed on top of a table. This board has wooden sides to prevent the marbles from rolling off the table.

In classrooms with water tables, the water table cover can be inverted and placed on a table to provide a quick setting for tabletop ramps. A preschooler actually used the empty water table as the site for ramps, with the sidewalls holding up one end of the ramp section and keeping the marble from rolling away. We also observed in classrooms where teachers attached bulletin board borders around a table to create a barrier for the marbles.

By limiting the materials and eliminating the time needed to retrieve marbles, the teacher created an activity (tabletop ramps) that allowed children to focus on what was happening with the incline and the marble. Tabletop ramps will not hold children's interest for long periods, so as interest wanes, children will need access to longer ramps, more marbles, and blocks for supports. Then the activity moves to the floor, giving children more space for their constructions.

Activity or Center Time

Another way to introduce ramps is to place materials in the ramp center and invite children to see what they can do. Dr. Christina Sales, a former preschool teacher, decided to simply place the ramp materials in the block center as a means of introduction. She limited materials to a few ramp sections of each size and several large and small marbles. She then observed to see how the 3-year-old children responded and adjusted materials as needed. If children did not use the ramp materials, Dr. Sales started to play with the materials herself and then asked the children if they wanted to join her. When children see the teacher working with ramps, they get the message that ramps are interesting; if an adult is playing with them, they must be important.

By placing ramps in the ramp center and inviting children to see what they can do with them, you are giving children the opportunity to follow their natural curiosity. They will explore ramps and find their own problems to solve. Children are tenacious in solving problems they set for themselves, often spending several days on the same problem. The teacher's role is to observe and intervene to promote deeper thinking, a part of making informed decisions in the ITM. In the next section, we discuss the use of *productive questions* as one way teachers can intervene.

TEACHER INTERVENTION

Comments and productive questions are two important strategies teachers can use to dig more deeply into children's thinking. Productive questions are questions that ask children to respond with more than *yes* or *no* answers, and to think more deeply about what they are planning or doing with ramps.

Teacher Comments

Productive questions are interventions designed to promote deeper thinking. Other good ways of intervening include just showing interest in what a child is doing by observing, providing hints to help children understand a concept, or remarking on events as they happen. For example, if a child has constructed a ramp that causes a marble to fall off before the end of the ramp, you might simply comment, "The marble fell off here," and then wait for the child to respond, either verbally or by changing the ramp structure. Then you could comment again about what the child is doing. This is called *parallel talk* and it maps students' action with language, providing opportunities to enhance vocabulary, as well as to model communication and extend students' comments (Pianta, La Paro, & Hamre, 2008).

Comments about children's ramp work should give them specific information about why they are correct or incorrect. Teachers should avoid using *Good job* or *Nice work* phrases, which are too generic. Children who repeatedly hear such phrases learn that the words are meaningless.

Children can also develop and promote self-explanation skills through questioning, using questions such as *What are you going to do next? What did you predict? What did you learn? How do you know?* Teachers can model these self-explanation skills through the use of *self-talk*, describing aloud what they are thinking or doing (Pianta et al., 2008).

ADULT–CHILD INTERACTIONS

Parallel talk is a strategy in which the adult verbally describes what the child is doing. The adult watches the child's actions and provides commentary without expecting a response from the child. The adult does not ask questions when using parallel talk (Pianta et al., 2008). Examples of parallel talk we observed during R&P activities include the following:

> "You put the marble in the middle of the ramp this time. Last time you put it at the top."
> "You took out the short ramp and added a long ramp, so now your structure is longer."

Self-talk is a strategy in which the adult verbally describes his or her own actions. No response from the child is expected. This strategy can be used to model self-reflection, questioning, and explanation talk (Pianta et al., 2008). An example of possible self-talk during R&P activities: "I'm going to put another block under this ramp section and see if the marble will go farther."

Feedback loops are back-and-forth exchanges between the adult and the child to help the child gain a deeper understanding of what is happening (Pianta et al., 2008). In feedback loops, the adult waits for the child to respond, then adds more information, asks a question, or restates what the child said using different words. The purpose is always to get the child to expand on his or her thinking.

Teachers should be wary of inserting their own agendas into the children's activities, especially when asking the higher-level productive questions below. Good observations will usually prevent this, unless the child is working on a task that is not clearly discernible to the teacher. Simply watching the child work can help, or the teacher may ask the child what he or she is trying to accomplish. Listening and responding in thoughtful ways will usually prevent or curtail teachers from moving children from their own agendas to the teacher's ideas. Those thoughtful responses will generate conversational *feedback loops* that strengthen communication skills as well as concept development (Pianta et al., 2008).

Teachers should save their agenda ideas for when the child is becoming disengaged or bored. Then providing a challenge, as described in Chapter 6, can revitalize children's interest.

Productive Questions

Productive questions were first introduced in the book *Primary Science: Taking the Plunge* by Wynne Harlen (2001). The book provides direct advice on how to support children's understandings through inquiry. In one chapter, Jos Elstgeest (2001) described types of good questions teachers should ask children. Productive questions are an effective tool to support inquiry teaching, boost confidence in both the teacher and children, and create a respectful environment in the classroom. But becoming an expert in asking productive questions takes time and practice.

Elstgeest (2001) described six different kinds of questions that are appropriate for upper elementary students. The questions are listed in a sequence that can help students move from the concrete to the abstract. With some modifications, the questions also work well with younger children. For example, younger children will not have an established sense of measurement using traditional instruments, and will do better if the measurement questions are more closely related to comparison questions (Fitzgerald & Dengler, 2010).

Once teachers understand the kinds of questions to ask, they need to consider timing. Moderation in questioning is important. Teachers must learn to avoid bombarding the children with questions, as well as waiting too long to ask a question. Deciding which question to ask at any one time is another challenge. However, using strong observation skills and a thoughtful approach will help teachers make these decisions.

Sometimes silence is as valuable as a good question. Just observing children at work on ramps can sometimes lead to conversations about the construction and problems the child may be experiencing.

We have experienced asking the wrong question, or asking a good question at the wrong time. Children will respond to a wrong question in a variety of ways. They may ignore you and continue working on their agenda, or they

PRODUCTIVE QUESTIONS

Below are listed six types of productive questions (developed by Elstgeest, 2001) along with examples of how they might be applied with R&P.

1. *Attention-focusing questions*—help students look specifically at a particular area of a ramp or at a specific object. Attention-focusing questions can help children consider a different perspective by focusing their observations.

   Sample Question: Where did the marble stop when it went up the second ramp?

2. *Measuring and counting questions*—ask students to quantify what happens. Quantifying and measuring for younger children will include nonstandard measurements or time frames. For example, using blocks or shoes to measure distance or a short song to measure time.

   Sample Question: How far did the marble travel after it hit the floor?

3. *Comparison questions*—help students contrast objects or events, or classify like things. Young children will notice similarities more than differences, so teachers should provide opportunities for children to locate characteristics or qualities that distinguish one ramp construction from another.

   Sample Question: Which marble went down the ramp faster?

4. *Action questions*—push students to try new ideas, or learn more about their current ideas. These questions can also be phrased as *I wonder* questions.

   Sample Question: What would happen if you added another block under the ramp?

5. *Problem-posing questions*—help students find and solve problems. For experienced ramp builders, these questions can spark new enthusiasm for exploring and eventually experimenting with R&P. For younger students, the child's agenda may take precedence over the teacher's ideas.

   Sample Question: What could you do to make the marble turn two corners?

6. *Reasoning questions*—help students verbalize their thinking by making sense of what they have experienced. Teachers should take care when asking students *why* questions, as young children

often do not know why, and will ascribe a particular event to magic or some illogical reason. Plus, teachers often ask *why* questions because they are seeking a specific correct answer. Asking, *Why do you think . . . ?* allows a child to answer with his or her current thinking, which gives teachers assessment information. It also allows the child to be correct, as his or her response to the question is a statement of current understanding.

Sample Question: Why do you think the marble stopped between the two ramps?

may walk away entirely. You will know when you have hit the mark when children engage in thoughtful responses, either verbally or by manipulating something in their ramp constructions. Teachers need to be willing to take these *psychological* risks in the same way that we want children to take risks in learning. *Wrong* questions for inquiry learning can include the following:

- Wordy, purely verbal or rhetorical questions
- Answers that can be found in textbooks, or one-right-answer questions
- Questions no one can answer, such as "Why are there lots of planets out there?"
- Questions that are too challenging for the developmental level of the children

Teacher–child interactions are the foundation of effective inquiry teaching and the ITM. How teachers intervene with their students during R&P activities can lead to positive adaptations of interactions throughout the curriculum.

APPENDIX 2.1. RAMP RELATIONSHIPS

From teacher Sherri Peterson's lesson plans, Freeburg Early Childhood Program, Waterloo, Iowa

- Relationship between the height of the marble run and the speed the marbles move
- Relationship between the slope of the ramp and the speed of the marble
- Relationship between the angle of the ramps and the speed of the marbles
- Relationship between the size of the marbles and the speed they roll
- Relationship between the foundation of the block structure and the height it maintains
- Relationship between the speed of the marble and the ease with which it rounds the corner
- Relationship between the weight of the target and the ease of knocking it over
- Relationship between the size of the ball and the number of targets knocked down
- Relationship between the shape of the object and the distance it moves
- Relationship between angle of the tubes and speed of the marbles
- Relationship between the placement of the tubes and the place the marbles land when they exit the tubes
- Relationship between speed of large marble and speed of small marble
- Relationship between speed of marbles and speed of micro-machines
- Relationship between slope and speed
- Relationship among the characteristics of an object (size, shape, weight) and the nature of the movement
- Relationship among the characteristics of an object (size, shape, weight, surface area) and the distance the object travels

APPENDIX 2.2. USING QUESTIONS WITH 1ST-GRADERS

Ramp Activities	Possible Questions
We have added a twist to the ramps in putting notches in the bottoms of the ramps along with a fulcrum. Students will have the opportunity to experiment with balance and weight by adding moving components to their marble run.	Where will your marble hit on this ramp? What do you want the marble to do on the ramp? Is there a special place you will need to put the ramp on the triangle? Will your ramp on the fulcrum change when the marble lands on it? Where will the marble go after that?
Previously: Ronald, Jose Luis, and Clayton worked together to make a ramp with one moving part that reversed the marble's direction. *Adaptations:* More ramps will be added to enable them to put more moving parts in their designs.	Where will your marble hit on this ramp? What do you want the marble to do on the ramp? Is there a special place you will need to put the ramp on the triangle? Will your ramp on the fulcrum change when the marble lands on it? Where will the marble go after that? Does it matter where you start your marble? Can you get another moving part into your design?
Students will have the opportunity to form relationships between the size and weight of marble and how it rolls down a ramp.	Which sphere rolls the farthest? What is it about this sphere that makes it go farther? Which sphere rolls the fastest? What is it about this sphere that makes it go fastest? Which is slower? Which goes the shortest distance? (and so forth)
Previously: The 1st-graders have been building linear ramps with jumps and drops. They have noticed that starting the marble higher up on the ramp allows the marble to travel with greater speed. They have found different starting places on their ramps to make the ramp successful. *Adaptations:* A challenge of building a ramp system up instead of out has been given. Students are to use the same size ramp pieces and unit blocks to build a ramp system inside a small rectangular area. In order for the ramp to be successful, they will have to pay attention to both the supports and the incline to adjust for the speed.	How many ramp pieces high can you build your system? Can you make just one ramp work? If you leave that ramp alone, can you build a ramp above it and connect the two so they both work?

CHAPTER 3

Physical Science Content and Inquiry

Lawrence Escalada

This chapter begins by expanding upon our previous definition of *science*. The *Next Generation Science Standards* and research are then revisited, followed by an expanded discussion of how to use the Inquiry Teaching Model to introduce physical science ideas and inquiry for all children. After identifying and defining the science inquiry processes related to the Ramps and Pathways (R&P) materials, we conclude by describing the essential physical science concepts that are inherent in R&P.

WHAT IS SCIENCE?

Science is the study of the natural world, including the laws of nature associated with physics, chemistry, biology, earth science, astronomy, and the application of facts, principles, concepts, or conventions associated with these disciplines. Physical science is the study of the physical world (nonliving materials) with the focus on physics, chemistry, earth science, and astronomy. Science is both a body of knowledge (content) and a way of knowing (process). It includes both science concepts and inquiry. Science is a way of knowing based on evidence using a variety of methods, including observation or experience, logical argument, and skeptical review. Sullenger (1999) points out that children are engaged in science in an elementary classroom when they do any of the following:

- They construct their own explanations and question their own and others' explanations.
- They talk and interact with others about their ideas.
- They make connections between their ideas and those accepted by others.
- They decide for themselves if the evidence provided is sufficient to accept their ideas.

Young children can engage in science. Although science involves many tools to collect, analyze, examine, evaluate, revise, and communicate information, these tools do not necessarily need to be sophisticated or complex. Engaging in science can be done anywhere and by anyone. Doing science is not restricted to individuals with white coats in laboratories with expensive equipment. Young children in and out of the classroom can engage in science. Now that we have expanded upon our definition of what science is, we will discuss what it means to be scientifically literate and what the NGSS and research recommend to develop literacy.

NEXT GENERATION SCIENCE STANDARDS AND RESEARCH

The NGSS (National Research Council, 2013) define a *scientifically literate individual* as one who understands and is able to apply science core ideas (content) as well as engage in science and engineering practices (inquiry) with the focus on crosscutting concepts across these disciplines to gain a broad perspective of these ideas. The two dimensions of the NGSS, science and engineering practices and crosscutting concepts, were discussed in Chapter 1. The third dimension includes the major ideas of the physical, life, and earth and space science disciplines in addition to engineering, technology, and application of science and the nature of science. The NGSS refer to these ideas as disciplinary core ideas (DCIs). Each DCI must meet at least two of the following for K–12 science instruction:

1. Address multiple sciences or engineering disciplines or be a key organizing principle of a single discipline.
2. Provide the means for understanding or investigating more complex ideas and solving problems.
3. Relate to student interests and real-life experiences or be connected to societal or personal issues that require an understanding of science or technology.
4. Ideas can be learned by younger students with greater sophistication and understanding in later years with further investigation.

Figure 3.1 identifies the core ideas and appropriate grade levels in the physical sciences applicable to R&P. These core ideas are related to performance expectations that students should know and be able to do to demonstrate that they have met the standards at various grade levels. For example, kindergarten children should be able to apply an understanding of the impact of different strengths or directions of pushes and pulls acting on an object—like a marble—by investigating its motion to analyze a design solution such as getting the marble to increase its speed by using a ramp (NGSS K-PS2 Motion and Stability: Forces and Interactions).

Second-graders should be able to make evidence-based decisions on how the different properties of matter are best suited to construct a ramp structure with individual blocks and ramps or break apart the structure to rebuild with a different purpose in mind (NGSS 2-PS1). Third-graders should be able to investigate the impact of balanced and unbalanced forces on the motion of an object, such as a marble on a ramp. These students can make observations and measurements of the marble's motion to provide evidence of pattern(s) that can be used to predict the future motion of the marble for different situations (NGSS 3-PS2). Fourth-graders should be able to use evidence collected to construct an explanation of the relationship between the speed of a marble and its energy. Students should be able to develop an understanding that energy can be transferred from a marble to a block when the marble collides with the block. They can apply their understanding of energy to design, test, and refine a ramp structure that converts energy from one form to another for a marble that moves through the structure (NGSS 4-PS3).

The NGSS use the term *scientific practices* to describe the major practices scientists use to investigate and build models and theories about the natural world. Scientific practices capture the essence of what is meant by inquiry in science and the various cognitive, social, and physical practices associated with inquiry (NRC, 2013). Students must be actively engaged in scientific practices. Engaging in these practices requires identification of assumptions, use of critical and logical thinking or reasoning, and considering and rethinking what one understands or knows with the possibility of alternative explanations. It must include opportunities for students to make logical arguments based on evidence. In elementary grades, students can develop the physical and intellectual abilities of scientific practices. These

Figure 3.1. Applicable NGSS Core Ideas in the Physical Sciences and Related Grade Levels

Physical Science		
PS1: Matter and its interactions (grade 2)	PS2: Motion and stability: forces and interactions (grades K, 3, & 5)	PS3: Energy (grades K, 4, & 5)
A. Structure and properties of matter	A. Force and motion B. Types of interactions C. Stability and instability in physical systems	A. Definitions of energy B. Conservation of energy and energy transfer C. Relationship between energy and forces D. Energy in chemical processes and everyday life

abilities include asking questions about objects and events in the environment, planning and conducting a simple investigation, using simple tools to gather data and extend the senses, using data to construct reasonable explanations, and communicating results and explanations. Although young children have difficulty with experimentation or investigation as a process of testing ideas and the logic of using evidence to formulate sophisticated explanations, they can still engage in many aspects of scientific practices.

The related physical science ideas found in R&P provide children with opportunities to consider and increase their understanding of the structure and properties of the objects and materials they experience daily. These properties must be observable and can include the type of material, size, mass (or weight), shape, color, and so on. Children can describe the position and motion of objects as well as manipulate the motion of these objects. As discussed in Chapter 1, the goal of the R&P materials is not to develop the conceptual understanding of basic physical science ideas (such as Newton's Laws) but to develop factual knowledge of these objects that is based on observations from direct experiences and investigations. This factual or practical knowledge can serve as a foundation or precursor to the conceptual understanding that will be developed later.

Young children can understand and engage in engineering practices in which they identify a simple problem, propose a solution, implement proposed solutions, evaluate a product or design, and communicate a problem, design, and solution. They can engage in engineering practices with R&P materials with opportunities that build on their natural curiosity to ask questions and investigate their surroundings. Young children can participate in these types of opportunities that engage them in scientific and engineering practices. The NGSS have provided us with guidelines on how to develop scientifically literate children. In the following section, we discuss how the physical science and science inquiry found in R&P relate to the Inquiry Teaching Model.

PHYSICAL SCIENCE AND THE INQUIRY TEACHING MODEL

The ITM was developed to capture the process of inquiry teaching (please reference Figure 1.1). It encompasses all of the important components of the teacher's role. Observation of children serves as the foundation of this model. The ITM is consistent with the recommendations of the *Next Generation Science Standards* in that children need to be actively engaged in scientific and engineering practices to develop an understanding of basic science ideas that can be applied across the disciplines of science and engineering with the focus of crosscutting concepts. Bybee (2013) recommends that translating the NGSS into classroom instruction must include an integrated instructional sequence of activities that includes active engagement and exploration. The Inquiry Teaching Model is our version of an instructional sequence of activities that is applicable to young children. With the focus on observation, the teacher can identify interests and prior ideas, skills, and experiences; activate learners' prior knowledge and experiences; stimulate interests; and capitalize on their natural curiosity. This approach is consistent with research on how students should learn and be taught science (Bransford, Brown, & Cocking, 1999). An educator may observe a child engaged in rolling a ball down the slide on the playground. This observation would inform the teacher that the child is curious about inclines and how objects move on them. The educator could then provide the child with a section of cove molding, a marble, and a tray, and ask the child to use the materials to get the marble to move. The child may push or blow the marble on the horizontal cove molding. He or she may raise one end of the track and release the marble from the top of the incline. This activity can serve to further stimulate children's curiosity about inclined planes.

After engaging the children, teachers can continue to observe what children do. These observations help the teacher make informed decisions to check for understanding, intervene to promote learning, integrate with other subjects, and document learning. Observations inform the teacher about what kinds of opportunities to provide in order to facilitate exploration, support problem solving, scaffold experimentation, and foster communication. Such opportunities involve STEM activities that are developmentally appropriate for young children to ask questions, define problems, investigate, and engage in other scientific and engineering practices.

Exploration in the ITM represents the most common opportunity for young children related to scientific practices as opposed to experimentation. Exploration is a self-directed, unstructured investigation with minimal teacher guidance. The exploration provides opportunities for children to interact with an object to determine its properties and how the object interacts with other objects. Children may observe patterns, identify variables, and establish possible relationships. Science process skills that are characteristic of scientific practices are used. It is important for children to communicate what they have observed, explain what they have done, and share what they understand.

An example of an exploration activity is one in which children are provided with a bucket; a bag of objects, including some that roll and some that don't roll (such as marbles of various sizes and masses or weights, jacks, dice, spools, cubes, plastic eggs, and so forth); three blocks or sponges; and a 1-foot section of cove molding. Children would be invited to play with the objects. The teacher would observe and note what the children do with the objects, occasionally probing with questions to determine what children are trying to do. This activity would continue with the teacher asking the children to investigate how the objects move down the incline. The teacher would continue to make observations and ask probing questions to challenge and help the children think about what they are doing. These strategies serve as formative assessments that allow the teacher to monitor and facilitate student learning (Keeley, 2008).

Problem solving within the context of engineering focuses on the design, redesign, and creation of human-made products. Similarly, we see children problem-solve as they self-direct their design and construct ramp structures (end products) in order to solve problems that interest them. In the process of solving a problem, children increasingly take into consideration what they know about how the world works. As children become more systematic in their problem solving, they construct new understandings about science, spatial reasoning, mathematics, language, art, and technological design, and use their new understandings in their problem-solving process. Our definition of problem solving, which utilizes concepts in science and mathematics, is consistent with the integration of scientific and engineering practices with crosscutting concepts found in the NGSS.

SCIENCE PROCESS SKILLS

Both exploration and experimentation in the ITM have components found within scientific inquiry. Scientific inquiry has been described in terms of processes (Ostlund, 1992) that are consistent with the scientific practices found in the NGSS. We use these processes to help define and differentiate between exploration and experimentation. The processes are described below within the context of R&P.

Observe—using one or more of the five senses to gather physical data or information. For example, a child can observe that a marble moves by releasing it from the top of a ramp.

Communicate—providing or engaging information verbally, graphically, through writing, and/or using body language. For example, a child can talk about how a car moves through his or her ramp structure: "It's a steep ramp. The car goes down then jumps off the ramp because it's going so fast." Nonverbal children can communicate through gestures (pointing to how the marble traveled), drawing, or writing about how their marble traveled.

Estimate—approximately determining a quantity or value based on judgment. A child can estimate how fast a marble moves down a ramp by making comparisons with marbles in other situations.

Measure—comparing objects using standard or self-defined units. A child can measure the distance a marble moves after leaving a ramp in terms of unit blocks. The child could also show with his or her hands held some distance apart how far the marble moved. Measurement does not have to include actual units of measurement. Young children who do not yet understand the concept of a unit may use qualitative terms such as *faster*, *slower*, *higher*, *lower*, *shorter*, *farther*, and so on to compare objects or events. Comparison is the beginning of measurement in early childhood.

Collect data—collecting information about observations and measurements. This may or may not be done systematically. A child can release a marble at different heights on a ramp and observe the differences in the distance traveled by the marble after leaving the ramp.

Classify—grouping or ordering objects according to some property or characteristic. This grouping or ordering of objects is based on observations. A child provided with a bag of different objects and a ramp will often divide the objects into two or more groups, based on whether and how they move down a ramp.

Infer—developing ideas based on observations. Inference requires judgment based on existing ideas and past experiences. For example, if a child observes two marbles released from the same height of the same ramp and one marble travels farther after leaving the ramp, the child may infer that one of the marbles is heavier than the other.

Predict—stating an idea of an expected result. Predictions are based on inference. A child may predict that a heavier marble may travel farther than a lighter one after being released from the same height on a ramp.

Make models—developing a physical or mental representation to explain an idea, object, or event. For young children, being able to look at a ramp structure, recognize that it will not work as constructed, and make the necessary changes to it before releasing a marble is evidence that the child has constructed a mental model (or representation) of the structure.

Interpret data—explaining information collected from observation and/ or reading tables, graphs, and diagrams, and/or using it to answer questions. See the example provided above for *Observe*: "When we put the ramp high then it makes everything go fast."

Hypothesize—stating a problem to be solved as a question to be answered by testing through experimentation. A possible relationship is tested— for example, the question, "What variable will determine the distance a marble travels after leaving a ramp?" A hypothesis is *not* a prediction or an educated guess. A hypothesis is a much more general idea that is used to design situations in which predictions can be made. The question provided above provides a framework to design possible experiments. As stated earlier, young children are generally not able to conduct formal experiments.

Control variables—manipulating one variable that may affect the outcome of an event while other factors are held constant. For example, if a child wants to determine the impact of changing the height from which a marble is released on a ramp on the distance it travels after leaving the ramp, he or she must keep other variables constant, including weight (or mass) and size of the marble, length of the ramp, steepness of the ramp, and so forth. Although young children may be able to see the necessity of controlling one variable, they generally do not understand how to recognize and control many variables.

Define operationally—stating information about an object, idea, or phenomenon based on experiences with it. For example, a child may use his or her own term (for example, *oomph*) to describe the force with which an object (such as a marble) hits another object (such as a block). Force may be described as a *push* or *pull*.

Figure 3.2 identifies the science process skills associated with exploration and experimentation from the ITM. Both involve investigations in which students use observations to collect and analyze information to draw conclusions to answer a question. Both involve the use of science process skills. Notice that experimentation involves more process skills, and that these additional skills require formal reasoning that is not required for an exploration. Depending on the investigation, young children may or may not be able to make inferences. The difference between exploration and experimentation is also how they are defined with R&P, based on how structured or formal the investigations are and whether or not they are self-directed or directed by the instructor. It should be noted that experimentation is not always teacher-directed.

Figure 3.2. Science Process Skills in Exploration and Experimentation

Science Process Skill	Exploration	Experimentation
Observe	✓	✓
Communicate	✓	✓
Estimate	✓	✓
Measure	✓	✓
Collect Data	✓	✓
Classify	✓	✓
Infer	?	✓
Predict	✓	✓
Make Models		✓
Interpret Data	✓	✓
Hypothesize		✓
Control Variables		✓
Define Operationally	✓	✓

We are defining experimentation with R&P as a teacher-guided, structured investigation in which students interact with the object(s) to collect and analyze physical data. The goal is for children to draw conclusions in order to answer a question. Most science process skills are used. Because young children are not developmentally ready to engage in sophisticated science inquiry, we recommend that young children be provided opportunities in which teachers scaffold the experimentation—opportunities that allow them to go beyond exploration.

Young children are not developmentally ready to engage in full scientific experimentation. It requires formal reasoning skills that do not develop until much later (Lawson, 2010). Taking a closer look at what qualifies as scientific experimentation may help us understand why and provide insights on how we can develop in young children the skills needed to go beyond exploration. With regard to R&P, scientific experimentation begins with the investigator identifying a research question or hypothesis related to the movement of objects on ramps—for example, "What variable will affect the distance a marble travels after leaving a ramp?" The next step would be to identify the possible variables and predict how changing these variables will impact distance. For example, the heavier the marble, the farther it will travel. The steeper the incline, the farther the marble will travel. The longer the incline, the farther the marble will travel. The investigator then identifies the variables. The *dependent variable* is defined as the variable that is affected—the distance the marble travels after leaving the ramp. The *independent variable* is defined as the variable that is manipulated or changed—the mass of the marble, steepness or slope of the incline, or the length of the incline. The *control variables* are defined as all other variables that must remain constant to establish a cause-and-effect relationship between the independent and dependent variables. The investigator then performs the experiment. Decisions are made about the procedures that will be used (how data will be collected and recorded and how observations will be made). Conclusions are made based on data, results, and evidence. For example, the heavier the ball, the farther it will travel after leaving the ramp. Results can be shared and discussed.

Although young children are not developmentally ready to engage in formal or sophisticated scientific experimentation and reasoning, they can and are eager to engage in scientific practices as described in the NGSS and the concrete reasoning that serves as a precursor to experimentation. It is important for the teacher to provide opportunities for students to engage in these practices that serve as a foundation for future scientific experimentation and understandings.

In addition to emphasizing opportunities for problem solving, exploration, and experimentation, ITM promotes ongoing communication. Communication is an essential aspect of children's active and successful engagement in scientific inquiry and problem solving during R&P. This will be discussed in more detail in the following chapter.

We have discussed the science inquiry aspect of R&P and how it relates to the ITM, but what about physical science content? This will be discussed next.

PHYSICAL SCIENCE CONTENT

R&P provides relevant and rigorous opportunities for young children to learn about physical science. Although young children are not able to learn about physical science concepts as a result of engaging in R&P activities due to the sophistication of these concepts, it helps if teachers have a foundational understanding of the underlying physical science concepts. The concepts to be addressed in this section include motion, forces and Newton's Laws, work and energy, forms of energy, and ramps and energy.

Motion

The motion of objects can be classified in terms of linear and rotational motion. If the object moves in a straight line, this is *linear motion*. A sliding block moving up or down a ramp undergoes linear motion. If the object rotates, it undergoes *rotational motion*. It is possible for an object to undergo both types of motion. For example, a rotating marble moving across the floor can both be rotating and moving in a straight line. A sliding block on smooth floor can move in one direction (*one-dimensional motion*) or a Hot Wheels car moving through a loop-the-loop can move in a curved path or circle (*two-dimensional motion*). In both one-dimensional and two-dimensional motion, the direction of the object can change. A bouncing ball can move down, stop, then up, and so on. A marble can move toward a block before it collides with it, stop, and then move away from it after the collision. A child on a merry-go-round can move in a circle. In addition to the direction(s) the object is moving, the motion of an object can also be described and classified by how fast or slow the object is moving. Is the object speeding up, slowing down, or moving steadily? Representations of the motion of an object can be provided in terms of words, values, symbols, pictures, diagrams, and graphs. Many of these representations, including mathematical symbols and equations as well as graphs, are not appropriate for young children. Formal terms such as *speed, velocity, acceleration, momentum*, and so forth are not appropriate either. The use of this terminology should be minimized or eliminated with young children. These terms are very abstract. They may have multiple meanings to different people and their use may reflect a lack of understanding of their correct meaning. The incorrect use of these terms by young children may convey misunderstandings that will be difficult to address as children get older. The emphasis should be placed on children's everyday language in describing the motion of objects on ramps. Students of all ages should be actively engaged in using their own words to describe and explain real-life physical phenomena in order for the experiences to help develop meaning and understanding (Cooney, Escalada, & Unruh, 2008; Robertson, 2002).

Instead of using the term *velocity*, the teacher could simply ask, "How fast is the marble moving? Is it moving fast or slow? Is the object speeding up or slowing down? What direction is it moving? Is it changing direction?" The distance an object travels in a given period of time can be used as a measure of how fast or slow an object moves. A faster-moving object travels a greater distance in a given period of time. If time is held constant, the distance an object moves can be used as an operational definition of how fast or slowly an object is moving.

The time it takes for an object to travel a given distance (like a runner or swimmer in a race) can also be used to measure how fast or slowly an object moves. A faster-moving object will travel the same distance as a slower-moving object but in less time. The measurement of time, however, is not easily observable without the use of tools such as stopwatches, especially if there are small differences in time. Young children find these tools difficult to use and understand. Therefore, it may make more sense with young children to focus on more observable results, such as the distance a marble travels after it leaves a ramp.

Children can explore linear or rotational motion of various objects. For example, a child can explore how a crayon slides down a ramp and compare its motion to the motion of other objects such as blocks, marbles, glass gems, and feathers. A child can add more blocks at the elevated end of the ramp to cause an object to slide down very quickly.

Forces and Newton's Laws

A *force* can be defined as a *push* or *pull* acting on an object. *Push* or *pull* are operational or working definitions of force. They provide a meaningful definition of force for the individual in that they trigger a connection to one's experience in exerting a force on an object. A force requires two objects to interact. For example, the action of a child kicking a ball involves both the ball and the child's foot. Two objects may interact by being in contact, or they may interact through a distance with no contact. When a child pushes a marble with his or her finger, the two interacting objects are the child's finger and marble. Because the child's finger and marble are in physical contact with each other, physicists call this a *contact interaction*.

When a marble is dropped from some height above the ground, the two interacting objects are the marble and Earth. Because the marble and Earth are *not* in physical contact with each other but are interacting through distance, physicists call this interaction a *noncontact interaction*. In this interaction, it is difficult to identify both interacting objects because we cannot "see" the Earth exerting a force in the same way we can see the child's finger exerting a force. The Earth, however, does pull on the marble, which results in the marble speeding up as it falls (see Photo 3.1). When a marble rolls down a ramp, the two interacting objects are the marble and Earth. This *noncontact interaction* is similar to a marble dropped from some height with the two objects being the marble and Earth, but it is different in that the marble is confined to moving down the ramp. The Earth, however, still "pulls" the marble so that it moves down the ramp.

Now that we have defined force, how is it related to the motion of objects? The relationship between forces and the motion of objects is governed by Newton's Laws. The First Law tells us that an object at rest remains at rest and an object in motion will continue to move steadily in a straight line unless acted upon by a *net force*. An object has *inertia*, or a tendency to resist changes in its state of motion or nonmotion. The *mass* of an object, or how heavy an object is, is a measure of an object's inertia. The more *inertia* an object has, the more resistance. For example, a child builds a ramp structure with a corner. She initially is unaware of Newton's First Law because

Photo 3.1. A Child Using the Earth to "Pull" a Marble Down a Ramp to Move Through a Structure that Includes a Corner Section

she does not place a block at the corner to cause the marble to change direction. She quickly corrects this problem after she observes that with nothing to block the marble's forward motion, the marble will continue to move in a straight line off the ramp.

Any object can have one or more forces acting on it. A child holding a marble in his or her hand is an example of two forces acting on the marble. The Earth pulls downward on the marble. This downward force is the *weight* (physicists call this force a *gravitational force*) of the marble. If the hand is not supporting the marble, we know that the marble will fall to the ground. The marble, however, does not fall to the ground because the child's hand is supporting it. In other words, the hand provides an upward force (physicists call this a *normal force*) that counters the downward force of Earth. These two forces that act on the marble are balanced in that when they are added together, the net sum is zero because the forces are equal in magnitude but act in opposite directions. If one or more forces acting on an object do not balance, the result is *net or unbalanced force* acting on the object. Imagine a stalled car that needs to be moved off the road. If the driver has two passengers, the two passengers can both push the car in the same direction to move the car off the road. The result is unbalanced forces or net force acting on the car. However, if they push the car in opposite directions with the same amount of force, the result is balanced forces acting on the car—no net force. The forces counter each other and the car doesn't move!

Photo 3.2. A Child Using Her Breath to Push, and the Earth to Pull, a Marble Down a Ramp

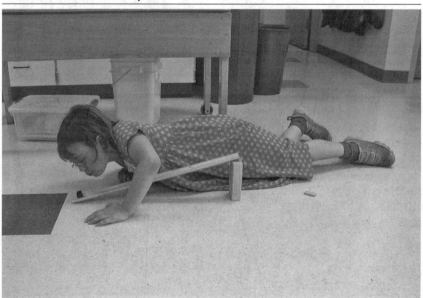

The Second Law tells us that a net force acting on an object will result in the object speeding up, slowing down, and/or changing direction. A block initially at rest can be made to move if a child blows on it in the right way with sufficient force (see Photo 3.2). A marble moving along a horizontal track can be made to stop, if the child pushes the marble with his or her finger in the opposite direction that it moves. Placing a container at the end of a ramp will stop the marble's movement (see Photo 3.3). By placing a block at the corner, children can cause the marble to turn a corner.

The Third Law tells us that for every action there is an equal but opposite reaction for two interacting objects. For example, a rolling marble hits a block. The *action* is the marble pushing on the block. The *reaction* is the block pushing the marble in the opposite direction. Recall that an interaction requires two objects. For every interaction, there is an action and reaction. Returning to the falling marble situation, recall that the two objects include the marble and Earth. The marble and Earth (ground) are some

Photo 3.3. A Child Using a Container at the Bottom of His Ramp Structure to Stop a Marble

distance from each other. As the marble falls, the action is the Earth pulling downward on the marble. The reaction is the marble pulling upward on the Earth. Notice that the action and reaction statements have the interacting objects switched, with the directions being reversed. But why does it not appear that the Earth moves since there is force acting on it? Recall that any object has resistance or inertia to changing its state of motion or rest. The Earth has a great deal of resistance because of its large mass! It should be noted that when the marble collides with the ground, both the marble and the ground push on each other in opposite directions. The upward push the ground exerts on the marble results in the marble coming to a stop because it was moving downward. The marble pushes downward on the ground (Earth) with the same force, but because the Earth has a large mass, or inertia, there is relatively no change in its motion or nonmotion.

Work and Energy

Work and *energy* are terms that we use all the time in our everyday lives. For example, we go to "work" and we consume "energy drinks" and "energy bars." Although we use the term *energy* a lot, it is not easy to define. As discussed earlier, objects interact with one another. A *system* of interacting objects may include a falling marble and the Earth or two marbles that collide. A system can also be as simple as a marble rolling down a ramp. Because the marble rolling down the ramp is being pulled by the Earth, the Earth must be included as part of the system. We will discuss more about why later.

Energy may be transformed from one form to the other. Some of the energy the system (of the ball and the Earth) has at rest at the top of the ramp changes to a different form of energy as the ball moves down the ramp. Some of the energy may not remain with the system of the ball and Earth over time. For example, a child pushes a stationary block on a smooth and horizontal table surface. The block moves but eventually comes to a stop. Work is done on the block during the child's push, resulting in the block moving from a state of rest. The work done provides the block with energy.

Every system in nature has energy including two objects that interact with each other. An example of two interacting objects is a marble that rolls down a ramp and the Earth that pulls the marble. Both the marble and the Earth have energy as the marble rolls down the ramp. A block on top of a ramp has energy (along with the Earth pulling on the marble). As it moves down the ramp, the marble moves faster. The marble (and the Earth pulling on the marble) at the top of the ramp and at any position along the ramp as it moves faster has energy. An empty Styrofoam cup standing upright is at the bottom of the ramp. The ball collides with the cup and knocks it over. The energy of the system of the ball and the Earth enables the ball to do work on the cup and knock it over. Unlike the everyday definition of *work*—a relative measure of the effort one puts into completing a task—work is done on an object when a net force acts on it and the object moves. The ball exerts a force on the Styrofoam cup when the two collide. The ball pushes the cup forward, causing it to move and fall down. Thus, work is done on the cup by the ball. Because there is an interaction between the ball and the cup, the Styrofoam cup also exerts a force on the ball as a result of Newton's Third Law. The ball continues to move but it slows down as a result of this force. Thus, work is also done on the ball by the cup. If the Styrofoam cup is replaced with a block of wood, the ball would slow down even more as a result of the collision. Work done on an object may result in the object speeding up or slowing down.

When a child stops pushing on a block, the block comes to a stop and it no longer has this energy. Where did the energy go? It has been transformed into a different form of energy that is no longer just associated with the block but is now associated with both the block and the table's surface. If you feel the bottom of the block and table's surface, you may notice that they feel warmer than before. This change in temperature is associated with a different form of energy.

Forms of Energy

The forms of energy relevant to R&P include the following:

> *Kinetic energy*—energy associated with a moving and/or rotating object
> *Potential energy*—stored energy associated with a system's relative position
> *Thermal energy*—energy related to the relative temperature of an object

All moving objects have *kinetic energy*. A marble that is initially at rest has no kinetic energy. A rotating marble, however, does have kinetic energy, as does a sliding block. The heavier an object and the faster it moves, the more kinetic energy it has. A heavy sliding block that moves as fast as a light sliding block will have more kinetic energy than the light one.

When two or more objects in a system interact, it is sometimes possible to store energy in the system in such a way that the energy can be recovered. This energy is called *potential energy*. It has the potential to be transformed into other forms of energy, such as kinetic or thermal energy. The greater the potential energy, the more energy can be transformed. The system of a marble held some height above the ground and the Earth has potential energy. The system of a marble on top of a ramp and the Earth has potential energy. The higher the marble is on a ramp, the more potential or stored energy the system of the marble and the Earth has. The type of potential energy associated with the position of an object relative to the Earth's surface, floor, table, or some reference level is called *gravitational potential energy*. The heavier an object and the higher it is positioned, the more gravitational potential energy the system has. A ball–Earth system of a heavy ball that is held at the same height as a lighter ball will have more gravitational potential energy than the lighter ball–Earth system. When talking about gravitational potential energy, the object and the Earth must be included in the system because they both interact with each other. A ball held at some height above the ground is being pulled downward by the Earth. The ball also pulls on the Earth but in the opposite direction. The ball and Earth act like two magnets that are attracted to each other (with the appropriate ends facing each other). Without the other magnet held some distance away, the magnets would not have potential energy. Without the Earth some distance away, the ball (and Earth) would not have gravitational potential energy. Imagine the ball far out in space with no nearby object, planet, or moon. The ball (and Earth) would not have gravitational potential energy (or would have very little) because there is no other object for the ball to interact with.

Thermal energy is the sum of the energies of the particles that make up an object related to their relative position and motion. It is related to how hot or cold an object is. Thermal energy is a relative measure of the *temperature* of the object. A hot object will have a greater temperature and thus more thermal energy than a cold object. Thermal energy is associated with an object or system of objects.

Ramps and Energy

Now that we have introduced the relevant forms of energy, we will illustrate how they are relevant to R&P. A ramp structure is constructed such that marbles are released from one end of a V-shaped set of ramps and travel to the other end (see Photo 3.4).

At the very top of the ramp, the system of the marble and Earth has the greatest amount of gravitational potential energy because the marble is at its highest position above the table or floor. As the marble moves down the incline, the amount of gravitational potential energy decreases for the system of the ball and the Earth. The marble, however, speeds up as it moves down the incline. The kinetic energy of the system increases as the marble moves down the incline. As a result, the gravitational potential energy of the system is transformed into kinetic energy. A marble that is released from the highest position on a ramp will travel farther after leaving the ramp because the system will have the largest amount of gravitational potential energy that gets transformed into kinetic energy. The more kinetic energy the system has at the bottom of the ramp, the faster the marble will travel at the bottom and thus the higher it will go on the other side. As the marble moves from one end of the V-shaped set of ramps to the other, a number of energy transformations take place:

Photo 3.4 Marble Moving Up and Down V-Shaped Ramp Structures

1. The marble rolls down the incline from some height (the gravitational potential energy of the marble and the Earth is transformed into kinetic energy).

2. The marble rolls up the opposite incline but does not travel as high as it was when it was released on the other side (kinetic energy is transformed into gravitational potential energy and thermal energy).

3. The marble rolls back down the opposite incline but does not travel as fast as it did previously (gravitational potential energy is transformed into kinetic energy and thermal energy).

4. The marble rolls up the original incline but does not travel as high as it did on the opposite incline (gravitational potential energy is transformed into kinetic energy and thermal energy).

The process repeats until the marble eventually comes to stop at the bottom of the V-shaped ramp formation. If the marble is at its lowest position relative to the table or floor and is not moving, the marble (and Earth) no longer have their original gravitational potential energy or their kinetic energy. Where did the energy go? According to the law of conservation of energy, energy can neither be created nor destroyed. If one form of energy in the marble system decreases, it must appear in an equal amount in another form, or it has somehow been transferred out of the system. Scientists consider the law of conservation of energy to be one of the most important laws of nature. The energy that the system of the marble and Earth once had went to both the marble and the ramps in the form of thermal energy, with some energy leaving the system. If the system of the marble and Earth is expanded to include the ramps, then the thermal energy for both the marble and ramps can be accounted for within the system. Unfortunately, the thermal energy cannot be recovered or used to change the position of the marble or cause it to move. The marble and ramps would have a slight increase in temperature as a result of the marble rolling back and forth on the ramps. This is very similar to rubbing your hands together, resulting in your hands feeling warm. The kinetic energy of the hands is transformed into thermal energy.

One way to make differences in gravitational potential energy for a system of objects and its impact more visible to children is to encourage them to investigate knocking down targets such as dominoes lined up one after the other at the base of a ramp. For example, when a marble is released from some height at the top of a ramp, the system of the marble and Earth starts out with a certain amount of gravitational potential energy that is transformed into kinetic energy as the marble travels down the ramp. When the marble reaches the bottom, it knocks down and moves some dominoes. But when the same marble is released at a lower height, the system of the marble and Earth starts out with less gravitational potential energy, which means that when the marble strikes the dominoes, it does so with less kinetic energy, and not as many dominoes fall over. The marble released from a lower height does less work on the dominoes. The same marble released from a greater height will result in more kinetic energy for the marble at the bottom. The marble will then exert a greater force on the dominoes that results in knocking more of them over. Thus, the marble now does more work on the dominoes, because more of them move and fall over. Although teachers should not use the terminology *gravitational potential energy* and *kinetic energy* with young children, they certainly can draw children's attention to the different results when the marble is released at different heights.

CONCLUSION

In this chapter we have identified and described the essential physical science concepts and inquiry processes related to the R&P materials within the context of the ITM that is consistent with NGSS. Young children can engage in aspects of scientific inquiry and learn about essential physical science ideas based on their experiences with R&P that serve as a precursor to formal scientific experimentation and developing a conceptual understanding of these ideas that can come later.

APPENDIX 3.1. DEFINITIONS OF PHYSICAL SCIENCE TERMS

Note: These formal terms are *not* appropriate for young children. These terms are provided for teachers.

Acceleration: change in speed and/or direction over a period of time. An object undergoes acceleration when it speeds up, slows down, and/or changes direction.

Contact interaction: two objects in contact with each other, resulting in a force acting on each object as a result of the other.

Distance: a measurement of the length an object moves.

Energy: a measure of an object or system's ability to do work. Comes in a variety of forms. May be transformed from one form to the other. Energy can be transferred from and into an object or system of objects.

Force: a push or pull acting on an object.

Friction: a force exerted on a moving object on a surface that resists motion, resulting from the interaction of the object and the surface.

Gravitational potential energy: stored energy associated with the position of an object relative to some reference level.

Heat: energy that is transferred from a hot object to a cold object. The transfer of energy that takes place due to a temperature difference.

Inertia: an object's resistance to change in its state of motion or nonmotion. Related to the mass or how heavy an object is.

Kinetic energy: energy associated with moving and/or rotating objects.

Linear motion: motion in one dimension or a straight line.

Mass: a measure of how heavy an object is and a measure of an object's inertia.

Momentum: the product of mass and velocity of an object. A heavier and faster object will have a greater momentum than a small and slower object. An object at rest has no momentum.

Noncontact interaction: two objects not in physical contact with other, resulting in a force acting on each object as a result of the other.

Potential energy: stored energy associated with an object's or system's relative position.

Rotational motion: motion associated with a rotating object.

Speed: measure of how fast or slow an object is moving. The average speed of an object is the total distance traveled over a period of time.

Temperature: measure of how hot or cold an object is.

Thermal energy: energy related to the relative temperature of an object. Sum of the energies of the particles that make up an object related to the particles relative position and motion.

Velocity: the speed of an object with direction.

Weight: the gravitational force acting on an object because of the celestial body (for example, the Earth) the object is on.

Work: force acting on an object through a distance, resulting in the object moving.

CHAPTER 4

Ramps and Pathways Promote Communication Development

Beth Van Meeteren

The thrills and challenges children experience when they engineer and build ramp systems produce an audible buzz as children share or exchange information, news, or ideas. Ramps and Pathways' STEM investigations become fertile ground for children to develop and use communication for a variety of purposes: to request additional materials, time, or space; problem-solve and share ideas; talk themselves through wicked problems; document; state a claim, explain, and argue; and celebrate success. This chapter explores ways teachers can create and work within a STEM environment that fosters the development of visual, verbal, and written forms of communication.

COMMUNICATION IS A CENTRAL STEM PRACTICE

To become proficient in science and engineering, students need opportunities to:

- ask questions and define problems;
- plan and carry out investigations;
- analyze and interpret data;
- construct explanations and design solutions;
- engage in argument from evidence; and
- obtain, evaluate, and communicate information (NRC, 2012).

Time spent on developing these practices positively affects children's learning (Bransford, Brown, & Cocking, 1999; Fox-Turnbull, 2010; Moll, 1992; Perret-Clermont, 1980). Establishing an expectation of negotiation in the classroom provides a tool for inquiry from the very beginning of a child's school experience. Kuhn and McDermott (2013) define *negotiation* in inquiry as a process whereby students make claims that are backed up with data and evidence and, as students' claims are challenged, students strengthen their argument with information from prior knowledge or data collected from the investigation.

R&P investigations compel young children to grapple with forms of Kuhn and McDermott's (2013) stages of negotiation: "self-negotiation," or verbalizing personal understandings of what they observe; "peer-to-peer negotiation," when students share and compare information with peers in small groups; and eventual "write to learn" behaviors of individually reflecting and recording what they have figured out. Negotiating within R&P demands that children communicate with many audiences such as peers, teachers, family, or classroom visitors through a variety of media.

Communicating to Cooperate

The development of children's communication is contingent upon the sociomoral atmosphere developed through the teacher–student relationship. In traditional classrooms, teachers often view themselves as the authority and direct the activities, rarely allowing students to make any decisions on their own. This results in a discourse pattern of call and response with the correct response determined by how closely it aligns with the teacher's thinking. However, as Piaget (1973) pointed out, such a classroom atmosphere produces intellectual and moral heteronomy, limiting students' ability to make their own decisions. Children become dependent upon the teacher and do not exercise their own thinking. They do not feel a need to communicate their ideas.

To enable children to develop problem-solving abilities and interest in communicating about those problems, Piaget recommended a shift from the traditional teacher–student relationship. In order for children to become confident and active problem-solvers, capable of explaining their thinking, Piaget insisted that teachers needed to provide opportunities to foster children's moral and intellectual autonomy. This includes the ability to take different perspectives into consideration and make decisions based on one's own thinking (Piaget, 1965). In this autonomous atmosphere, the teacher considers the children's points of view and encourages them to consider one another's (DeVries & Zan, 2012). Children experience a dialogic classroom where they learn patterns of language to cooperate, state a claim, negotiate in scientific discourse, and come to consensus (Johnston, 2012).

A way to begin sharing decisionmaking is to include children in rule-making (Geiken, Van Meeteren, & Kato, 2009) or setting guidelines in building R&P. This requires the teacher to maintain a leadership role as he or she guides the process by asking, "How can we work within this space to build ramps? What kinds of things do you think will keep everyone happy and working?" As children contribute, the teacher can continue to probe, asking children to expand and clarify, modeling a desire to understand and value ideas.

You said we should write "be kind to each other." What would that look like in the Ramps and Pathways center?

Asking for clarification helps the children examine the center and its operation from their perspective and take ownership. It also implies that the teacher has confidence in the children's ability to regulate and operate the center.

The ideas are written in children's words on chart paper. Every child has a vested interest in what is recorded and is finely attuned to and interested in how to express opinions and ideas in writing. Rule-making becomes a productive interactive writing session where children pay close attention to how their speech can be represented in print.

Because children are the creators of the guidelines, they ensure that the guidelines are followed. We have seen many occasions where children have pulled peers over to where the rules are posted and read them aloud when there has been a disagreement. When further complications in the center demand reworking a guideline, children experience their role in writing amendments. Children are immersed in the act of writing for a specific purpose and audience as well as the writing process of drafting, revising, editing, polishing, and publishing (Graves, 1994).

Working together promotes perseverance and autonomy. Work conversations can help children develop perseverance and autonomy when they encounter challenges. To scaffold a child who is becoming frustrated with lack of success, the teacher can model using self-talk to deal with frustration:

It sure is frustrating when it's not working, but you are still looking closely to see what is happening so you can fix it. You are not giving up!

Other times, the teacher can make a suggestion to persuade the child to examine a problem from another perspective:

It doesn't seem to be working that way. I wonder if it would make a difference if you tried something else.

I wonder if you looked at the structure from this angle if you can see what is going wrong.

Times of frustration can provide perfect opportunities to introduce and nurture collaborative thinking to solve problems. The teacher can cultivate these collaborations by making suggestions such as these:

I remember last week Joe had the same kind of problem. Do you suppose you could ask him to take a look at this to see what he did to solve the problem?

Have you noticed anyone else who may be able to help you figure this out? Is there a way you could get them to help? Would you like me to help you ask them?

When the teacher helps children understand that it is okay to ask for help, they find it is beneficial to work and learn as a team. Doing so builds a learning community where problems are a natural part of learning for everyone and a supportive community of learners is available to help solve those problems.

Executive function and project work. Coordinating the designing and building of R&P systems demands sophisticated development of the executive functions of inhibitory control, working memory, and cognitive flexibility. The development of executive functions plays a crucial role in success in literacy, mathematics, and later STEM learning (Blair & Razza, 2007; Brock, Rimm-Kaufman, Nathanson, & Grimm, 2009; Diamond, 2013; Shaul & Schwartz, 2014).

R&P experiences are much like project work (Katz & Chard, 2000) and provide children with a common focus, motivation, and opportunities for conversation where vocabulary and language is enhanced (Beneke, 2010). By providing more opportunities for conversations around these experiences, we enable children to develop deeper conceptual understanding and a large and richly structured vocabulary at an early age, which can support their reading comprehension skills in later grades (Mol & Neuman, 2014).

Promoting Talk During Ramps and Pathways

Children are compelled to engage in self-talk and verbal exchanges when they design and build ramps. This is encouraged in dialogic classrooms by teachers who understand the importance of talk in developing vocabulary and language patterns. The research of Hart and Risley (2003) pointed out the role of adult–child verbal interaction in establishing vocabulary and language patterns. Prior to school, children develop vocabulary, language, and interaction styles similar to those of their caregivers that may or may not match the language of the child's school culture. The child's home language experiences differ not only in terms of number and kinds of words heard, but also in regard to language that encourages, or discourages, independent thinking and learning. Hart and Risley's study concluded that educational interventions must not only address lack of knowledge or skill in using the school's cultural language, but must also consider experiences that encourage habits of seeking, noticing, and incorporating more complex experiences, all essential to developing scientific and engineering practices (NRC, 2013). R&P provides the perfect venue for such language development.

As teachers observe children building, they may collect language samples. Analysis may reveal increasing lengths of utterances, and teachers can track oral language development (Clay, 2005). Analysis also reveals a child's preconceptions about how the world works: precursors to understanding physics. Informed with this nuanced understanding of the child, the teacher can intervene with meaningful comments to expand the child's vocabulary and conceptual understanding:

- I notice your marble rolls quickly on the steep ramp, or the ramp that has one end much higher.
- I see you chose to use a heavy marble, a marble with more weight to it. It seems to be rolling farther than the lighter marble.
- You seem to be building your structure to be stable and sturdy. It doesn't fall or collapse when you lean on your ramp.

When teachers provide specific feedback on children's work, children are more apt to respond and continue conversations with the teacher and peers, thus improving their skills in communication. For example, at the beginning of the year in my 1st-grade classroom, I observed Alex creating a slope or incline that caused a marble to move down a track. In conversation with me he said, "When I bend the track, the marble rolls down." Alex lacked a word to describe the incline. Working nearby, Shayla joined the conversation, using the world *tilt* in the context of the incline. Soon, Alex was using the word *tilt* in place of *bend*. In a dialogic classroom, or a classroom where conversations are expected and nurtured, children are free to talk with other children as they work. Within these conversations, children expand on one another's word usage, vocabularies, and quality of phrasing.

This is equally true for native English speakers as well as dual-language learners (DLLs) (Cohen & Uhry, 2007; Fawcett & Garton, 2005; Mashburn, Justice, Downer, & Pianta, 2009). Teachers in the United States as well as in countries abroad have told us that R&P experiences were of great benefit to DLL students (see also Chapter 5).

While engaging in communication with young children, it is important to remember that understanding one another is the primary goal. The introduction of complex vocabulary should serve to expand this understanding, not create barriers. We recommend refraining from using scientific language that the children do not conceptually understand. Avoid words like *acceleration*, *momentum*, and *velocity* because terminology can have different meanings for different people, and may be inconsistent with the definitions of the scientific community. It is also wise to stay away from statements like "Friction makes the marble slow down." Nobel Prize–winning physicist Richard Feynman (1985) was frustrated with how science textbooks asked children to memorize correct answers such as "Energy makes it move." Such answers are hollow and empty of meaning. Instead, Feynman suggested teaching children to describe what they observe in their own language. For example, a teacher could say, "Tell me what you notice about how the marble is moving." Children can answer with their own words with definitions they understand: "The marble is slowing down because it keeps bumping into the bumps on the carpet." Once they have a deep understanding of what is going on, children can be introduced to the term *friction* and how it is related to the interaction of the marble and the carpet as the marble rolls across the carpet.

Communicating to Share Ideas and Problem-Solve

Professional scientists and engineers draw upon a vast network of knowledge and expertise they have amassed throughout their education and careers in preparing for their next research plan and project. Because of this, they have developed efficient protocols or systems to communicate with one another to use time and materials wisely. In engineering, this is known as the engineering design process. When professional engineers are given a job to do, their first task is to communicate with one another to identify the needs and constraints of the job. They determine what has already been done, and they develop possible solutions. Using their knowledge and expertise in physics and properties of materials to determine what they believe is the best solution, they build a prototype and test, evaluate, and improve the design as needed. Engineers do not use the engineering design process in a linear fashion, but rather enter in and out of phases intermittently as the project demands.

Attempts to include engineering in K–12 has resulted in a simplified definition of the engineering design process. Although the simplified engineering design process may work with older students, holding preschool and primary grade children accountable to it is extremely problematic. Young children are still self-negotiating and verbalizing what they observe and understand about how the world works. They have not had enough experiences to acquire the knowledge and expertise or even yet developed the cognitive capacity to consider all the constraints, brainstorm multiple ideas, and select the best one. Children's excitement about creating, testing, and improving their ideas helps inform their understanding of how the world of objects works (Van Meeteren, 2013).

Communication within these experiences allows young children to acquire the necessary knowledge and expertise to engage in more formal engineering behaviors in later grades. Until then, it is more essential for the teacher to use conversation to develop self-negotiated concepts about how the world works. Through conversation, the teacher can model wondering, noticing details, and encouraging the child to slow down and reflect upon the reasoning that went into the building of the structure. The child's conceptual understanding can be observed and recorded by the teacher. Educating the teacher on the workings of the structure, the child develops a sense of confidence and accomplishment.

As the center operates, the children's developing ideas are powerful opportunities to help the children engage in scientific discourse. At least twice a week or more, we found children were interested in discussing ideas about ramp structures as a whole class. Sometimes these discussions were impromptu and took place when a powerful discovery was made; other times they were used as content for mini-lessons about writing. Both served as prime opportunities to engage in literacy development.

When children made a discovery in constructing or engineering a ramp structure, or encountered a perplexing problem, we would often gather around the structure itself. The builders were urged to present their structure and their idea or the problem they were trying to overcome. The teacher's role was to help moderate discussion and provide models for disagreement that would help children look at problems from different points of view and not escalate into personal arguments. This often meant the teacher rephrased statements for the children.

USING QUESTIONING TO HELP MODERATE DISCUSSION AND DISSENTING OPINIONS

The following exchange between a teacher and a child demonstrates how the teacher asked questions and rephrased the child's statements to help guide and facilitate perspective taking as children solve problems during ramp construction.

Juanita: You wrong! That's not going to work.

Teacher: You mean you disagree with how the ramp structure is arranged? Tell us why you disagree with the construction. What problem do you see happening?

Juanita: You can see that won't work.

Teacher: You can see something wrong from where you are standing? I wonder if we got behind you and looked at it from the same place you are looking at, if that would help us see something different. Let's try.

Teacher to builder: What do you think? Do you see something you might need to adjust? Do you agree with Juanita that it won't work? Isn't it interesting how looking at the problem from another angle can give us such different ideas? Thanks for pointing that out, Juanita.

Through the teacher's modeling of how to politely disagree and express dissenting opinions, the children learned to use language that permitted peers to observe more closely or from different perspectives. There were more exchanges and attempts to clarify ideas rather than attempts to over-power. They were a united community of learners engaged in deep investiga-tion to make sense of how the world works.

Many times, as children explained how their ramp structures worked, they would offer generalizations within their explanations. These could be turned into discussions where they could engage in scientific argumentation.

In this way, the teacher works to help children both explain how they are thinking as well as consider ways to argue their thinking. Eventually, they will come to see that speed and the degree of the incline are related and that they are both right. The steeper the incline, the faster and farther the marble will travel. It also introduces the idea of creating diagrams and using draw-ings to represent and communicate thinking. This encourages attention and

---

DISCUSSION USED TO ENGAGE SCIENTIFIC ARGUMENTATION

The following discussion illustrates how children can actively engage in scientific argumentation.

Moira: If you want the marble to go all the way to the end, you have to make the first ramp steep.

Teacher: Are you saying that a steeper ramp makes the marble go farther?

Moira: Yes. The steeper, the farther.

Kajeil: I disagree. I think the faster the marble goes, the farther it goes.

Tiamarah: Well, if it is steeper, the marble *will* go faster too.

Teacher: I'm starting to get lost. Let's try to organize our thinking. Moira, you first said for the marble to roll all the way to the end, the first ramp has to be steep. Can you draw on this paper what a steep ramp would look like?

Moira draws.

Teacher: About how many blocks do you suppose it would take to make the ramp that steep? Could we hold a block up to the drawing to get an idea?

Moira holds up a unit block to the drawing.

Teacher: I'm wondering if we make a mark here to show a unit block, we can draw some more marks to show how many unit blocks we are using. Do you think people looking at this are going to know these are blocks? Let's try labeling them "blocks." I'll draw a line from the word to the marks so they know what that is . . .

use of informational text, a genre that is far too absent from early childhood classrooms (Duke, 2000) and a genre that is problematic for many readers in later grades. Early exposure to informational text in authentic contexts helps children learn how informational text works and why it is necessary.

Communicating STEM Ideas Through Writing and Reading Tasks

Literacy skill acquisition plays a dominant role in early childhood curriculum. R&P provides an authentic context for children to learn to write and read as they document what they are doing and thinking. This documentation can take the form of sketches, digital photos, video, or writing created by children or co-created with their teachers.

Even before children understand the alphabetic principle, they are eager to communicate their ideas about ramp structures. Occasionally, children will spontaneously draw their ramp structures. Teachers can capitalize on these occasions by talking with children about their drawings and use the opportunity to introduce children to informational text. After asking permission to label parts of the drawing with the child's help, the teacher can ask the child about specific parts of the drawing and the functions of each part. For example, the teacher could say:

> I see you have quite a few parts to your structure. Can you show me where I would put the marble to start? Is it okay if I write "start" here so I can remember? Let's see . . . "start" begins with the /s/ sound. . . . Help me remember what letter makes the /s/ sound.

The teacher can slowly enunciate each phoneme while writing its grapheme. Pointing to the completed word, the teacher and student can read it together. In this way, the teacher models that print has meaning, written words represent spoken words, and certain symbols represent certain sounds in our speech. These repeated experiences help children develop the concept of the alphabetic principle and they soon begin to experiment with recording their own thoughts.

Ramp structure photos. We found that taking pictures of children as they build and printing out single photos or a series of photos highly motivates children to reflect and write about their work. This documentation can take many forms. Single pictures may be used as opportunities to label the child's work in the same way the child's drawing can be labeled.

Child interviews. Another way to use single pictures is to interview the child about the picture. Be sure to be selective when asking interview questions. You want to scaffold the child's learning and development, so timing is important. Asking too many questions would exhaust the child as well as prevent the student from continuing to work, so we recommend choosing only a few. It is equally critical for the teacher to interview children about their ramp structures using a relaxed, nonthreatening approach.

Conducting an interview does several things. First, it brings honor to the child's work and enables teachers to demonstrate that they value the child's work and thinking. Second, it puts the child into the position of reflecting on his or her work and engaging in metacognition, or thinking about his or her thinking. Third, it provides teachers with a window into children's conceptual understanding of how the world works and informs teachers about how they can improve the educational environment to accommodate children's needs. Fourth, it provides an opportunity for an authentic literacy lesson about the importance of including details in writing.

After the short interview, the teacher could invite the child to write about the picture to help the teacher remember the conversation. Another audience could be the child's family. A third audience could be classmates who may want to rebuild the structure. Offering different audiences for the child's writing requires the child to think from the perspective of the reading audience to determine the most important things to include in the piece.

If the child is still developing the alphabetic principle, the child can dictate to the teacher and the teacher acts as a scribe. If the child is developing sound/symbol relationships, the child can write on the page. The teacher can use this moment to celebrate what the child understands about how

---

SAMPLE INTERVIEW STATEMENTS AND QUESTIONS

Tell me what you are trying to do in this picture.

Help me understand what you are trying to get to happen in your structure.

Tell me what is working in your structure.

Tell me about the problems you had/are having in your structure.

How do you solve those problems?

Did anyone give some helpful suggestions for building?

Tell me about how you got the idea for your structure.

How did you start?

What was the hardest part?

What surprises did you have?

What part do you think is the most interesting?

Can you help me understand what this part does?

Can you help me understand what will happen when the marble goes here?

What do you plan to try next?

Are there any different kinds of materials you wish you had available?

print works, pointing out the child's conventional uses of beginning and/or ending sounds in the writing. Teachers can then challenge the child to think a bit harder about one specific feature of the writing, nudging him or her closer to conventions of writing and spelling.

The interview could also be completely verbal, recorded and possibly shared on a classroom wiki through a podcast or through email with family members. Another possibility is to collect video footage of the construction and presentation of a ramp structure. This could be uploaded to a platform such as VoiceThread, a web-based digital storytelling application that allows users to share photos, videos, text, and audio, and allows visitors to comment on the work through voice with a microphone, telephone, text, audio file, or video with a webcam. VoiceThreads can be shared with anyone in the world or kept private for a selected audience. It is a wonderful way to share a child's learning with parents and family members.

Ramps and Pathways Documentation Boards

Uninformed observers of a classroom engaged in R&P may be confused and even dismissive of the children. A way to educate these observers is to construct documentation boards to tell the story, purpose, and conceptual development involved in R&P activities. In the process, teachers gain even more insight into the children's conceptual knowledge and can use it for both formative and summative assessment. Also, if children are involved in creating the documentation, they gain even more authentic experiences with literacy.

Katz and Chard (1996) recommend that documentation include not just a presentation of the final product, but samples of the child's work in progress. Written comments by the teacher or other adults can highlight important discoveries the children made along the way. Transcriptions of children's discussions and comments and photos reveal how their conceptual understanding continued to develop (see Photo 4.1). The collection of documents on display reveal how the children planned, carried out, and completed the work (Katz & Chard, 1996).

As mentioned earlier, media such as VoiceThread enable teachers to create web-based documentation that can be shared with audiences beyond the physical classroom. However, we recommend creating documentation boards within the classroom or in the hallway as well. Such boards are a visible reminder to the teacher and students of the importance of the work they are doing. They can serve as a tool in reviewing and reflecting on earlier work, and planning new directions as well as providing additional practice in reading and writing. Collaborating with the children in creating a documentation board on a classroom bulletin board or in the hallway can help them tell the story of their rigorous work in R&P. Artifacts and evidence can highlight conceptual development in physics as well as behaviors and habits in creative design and engineering.

Photo 4.1. Teacher Observes a Child's Strategy in Designing and Building a Support Structure

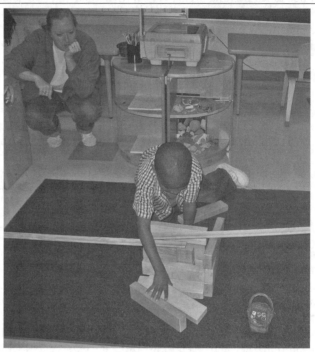

Creating a successful documentation board requires the teacher to consider the audience and purpose (Seitz, 2008). For example, if the teacher wants to illustrate how R&P aligns with math, science, engineering, and technology standards, he or she will select samples of children's work that highlight this alignment. This could include photographs of children counting blocks to measure height or weighing spheres to compare weight, along with children's comments and background information on how they used measurement to communicate within their R&P investigations.

If the desire is to illustrate pre-engineering thinking, a series of photographs documenting the evolution of a ramp system with written explanations of conceptual thinking at each stage of building is a powerful way to inform visitors of the rich learning involved. Collaborative creation of a documentation board can serve two purposes. First, it clearly explains the overall objective and value of R&P. Second, as children reflect on their learning, they describe their thought processes, providing further opportunity to deepen their conceptual understandings and creating yet another authentic context for developing literacy skills.

Readers and Writers Authentically Communicate About R&P

With increased attention to literacy scores in standardized tests, teachers and administrators may be reluctant to devote so much time, attention, and space to STEM activities such as R&P. By now, the reader should already have constructed how literacy learning is deeply embedded in integrated STEM investigations. STEM investigations support and enhance literacy development.

We have found that when children engage in R&P in a supportive environment, they learn to expect problems and expect to figure them out. They are open to taking risks in their work, expecting to learn from mistakes. This healthy respect for learning from mistakes transfers to literacy learning. Just as children become comfortable encountering problems in engineering their ramp structures and learning patterns in how the laws of physics work, they become comfortable encountering problems in their uses of literacy and learning patterns in how speech and print work. There is no longer an unrealistic expectation that everything they speak, read, and write must be perfect the first time; instead, they gain an understanding that learning to read and write and speak is a process that allows them to revise and refine their knowledge and use of literacy over time.

In far too many pre-K, kindergarten, and primary classrooms, performance in literacy is what defines a child's success, because literacy is what is evaluated at the state level in early childhood. When the school environment is so heavily focused on the domain of literacy and children are restricted to one literacy activity after another throughout the school day, children who struggle but possess strengths in early STEM come to learn that their knowledge, expertise, and ideas are not valued or important. These creative children may find solace in activities such as block building offered at free choice time (which is becoming increasingly rare, even in kindergarten). However, the block center is seldom valued by the school culture and, if allowed, it is viewed as a way to keep children occupied until the teacher can do the important academic work with them in small-group instruction (Casey, Andrews, Schindler, Kersh, & Samper, 2008).

When they are offered experiences such as Ramps and Pathways, all children find a way to experience and celebrate success. Furthermore, we have found that children who languished in literacy early in the year, but experienced success in R&P, became motivated to learn the patterns of language to communicate their ideas, problems, and success with others. They work to develop conventions of Standard English in order to be understood. They acquire and use vocabulary specific to informational texts. Ramps and Pathways challenges children to learn to read and write a variety of text structures and develop foundational skills in print concepts, phonological awareness, phonics, word recognition, and fluency. Children write *lists* of materials they need, *directions* (procedural writing) for others to follow, *signs* to inform onlookers to look, but not touch. They *sequence events* as they order and *describe* a series of pictures of their work. They write to reflect, debate, and record ideas within a community of learners.

CONCLUSION

The engaging work of Ramps and Pathways creates an atmosphere where children are hungry for ways to share ideas. Often, these ideas involve science and engineering concepts that are relevant and meaningful to the children. Actually doing science and engineering requires use of mathematics, and skills in listening, speaking, reading, writing, and viewing to communicate effectively. In this way, content domains are fully integrated to where they are most meaningful and relevant to young learners (Kamii, Miyakawa, & Kato, 2004).

Many teachers may be reluctant to give up instructional time in literacy to allow children to experience the R&P curriculum. Instead of robbing the literacy instructional block, we found that Ramps and Pathways breathed life into the act of literacy itself. Children did not ignore literacy activities but rather demanded them in order to bolster their communication skills and share their R&P experiences with others. As an unexpected bonus, we found the increased perseverance that developed through R&P activities served children well and helped support their literacy development. As children became accustomed to their ramp structures not working the first time and trying something different to get them to work, they became accustomed to making mistakes in reading and writing, trying a different approach to make something work or make sense.

The inquiry skills children developed during R&P seemed to spill over into reasoning in reading comprehension and mathematics, agreeing with research that parallels science and literacy concepts (Cervetti, Pearson, Bravo, & Barber, 2006; DeVries & Sales, 2011; Padilla, Muth, & Lund Padilla, 1991; Yore, Bisanz, & Hand, 2003). Further discussion on STEM integration will be provided in Chapter 6.

CHAPTER 5

Using Ramps in Diverse Learning Communities

Shelly Counsell and Melissa Sander

Early science experiences like Ramps and Pathways (R&P) promote young children's cognitive development, including children with special needs. Of all the academic domains, science may be the one that can be most easily adapted for students with disabilities. R&P provides the kind of authentic, open-ended early science activities with hands-on multisensory materials and rich opportunities for groupwork that are easily adaptable for young children with disabilities.

Since the 1970s, few studies have examined the participation of students with special needs in inquiry-based learning in science. This is partly due to traditional assumptions that these learners must first memorize science facts and conceptual knowledge (using a noninquiry, text-based approach) before they will benefit from inquiry-based instruction (Carlisle & Chang, 1996; Gersten & Baker, 1998). Even fewer studies (for example, Rapp, 2005) have investigated inquiry science learning with students who require extensive supports (Spooner, DiBiase, & Courtade-Little, 2006), suggesting that inquiry experiences are of little value to learners with severe cognitive delays, as they are seen as intellectually inferior. Female students, students of color, and students considered dual-language learners (DLLs) are frequently viewed as intellectually inferior as well (Atwater, 1996). Too often, these students are left out of science inquiry experiences to concentrate on the basics of reading, writing, and arithmetic.

As early educators who have worked with the full range of learners, we operate on the overarching premise that if *all* learners are to gain access to, fully participate in, and achieve maximum profit from early science opportunities, educators need to understand, believe in, and value science as a learning experience for *all children*. Valuing science as a learning experience for all children requires educators to view all children as *science learners*. The rallying cry declaring "science for all" has recently gained increasing attention, transforming this movement into a national goal for public education (American Association for the Advancement of Science, 1991; Howe, 2002; National Research Council, 2007).

In this chapter, we challenge teachers to consider the full range of learners as they ponder implementing R&P. This includes young children labeled as gifted and talented, children who are DLLs, and children with disabilities. To help educators successfully implement R&P with the full range of learners, this chapter demonstrates that R&P (1) is an effective universally designed learning (UDL) curriculum; (2) is an open, flexible curriculum, easily integrated with evidence-based practice; and (3) addresses children's individual learning rates, strengths, and needs when combined with the necessary accommodations and modifications across the different developmental domains and academic content areas.

We actively embrace the view that all children fall along a continuum of human development, skills, talents, temperaments, interests, abilities, cultural backgrounds, and life experiences. These attributes, combined with a child's learning rates, strengths, and needs across developmental domains and academic content areas, form a complete developmental composite that represents the child's learning profile. Focusing on what is educationally relevant, rather than categorically ranking and sorting children based on deficit assumptions, is not only sensitive and respectful to the individual learner, but it likewise increases children's access to learning activities through varied instruction (and intervention).

Universal access to learning and instruction achieved by science activities such as R&P diminishes the discriminatory and damaging effects caused by academic tracking and homogeneous ability grouping practices. The following discussion provides some helpful, general recommendations intended to guide and enhance children's access to and engagement in R&P activities. Parents, caregivers, and educators should never ignore or neglect relevant educational factors and considerations pertaining to individual children's aptitudes, language development, and disabilities. At the same time, it is imperative to avoid overgeneralizing or stereotyping learners in ways that can impede or limit learning opportunities.

As the guiding framework, the Inquiry Teaching Model (ITM) can help support early childhood professionals in implementing R&P activities with the full range of learners. Based on the ITM, this chapter helps educators specifically develop strategies to (1) engage diverse learners as science participants; (2) create science opportunities for diverse learners; (3) accommodate developmental considerations during science activities; and (4) connect science with literacy, math, and engineering skills.

ENGAGING DIVERSE LEARNERS AS FULL PARTICIPANTS IN SCIENCE LEARNING

To ensure children gain full access to and engagement in R&P activities, teachers must share in their commitment to and expectation that *all* children can learn and participate in science. "An accessible curriculum," according to the Council of Exceptional Children's Division of Early Childhood (DEC), is one in which "all aspects of the curriculum (e.g., environment, activities, materials) invite active participation of all children, regardless of disability or special needs" (2007, p. 4). An effective UDL curriculum, as recommended by Rose and Meyer (2002), provides flexible, customizable, child-centered, child-directed activities that are highly accessible to all learners—like R&P.

Accommodations and modifications are likewise implemented to further address and enhance R&P's universal design with the full range of learners. Accommodations are individualized changes or adjustments made to maximize the children's access and participation. Possible accommodations include altering or varying ramp materials, allowing children to use various response formats (including augmentative and alternative communication systems) and varying the physical arrangement in the learning environment.

Similar to accommodations, modifications to practices and expectations are determined on an individual basis to support the different learning styles and needs of diverse learners working with R&P. Possible modifications include changes in the instructional level, content, and performance criteria, as well as varying assessment procedures and using alternative assessments.

As a universally designed curriculum, R&P activities can easily be implemented with children classified as gifted and talented, DLLs, or children with disabilities. The following discussion is intended as a starting point, a place of departure, and a point of reference only. Use this information as a guiding framework to inform R&P instructional planning and implementation with young children, not as the end-all or be-all that could potentially limit, hinder, or impede children's access because of biased assumptions.

Children Considered Gifted and Talented

Children are identified and placed in programs for gifted and talented learners based largely on grade point averages and standard intelligent quotient (IQ) scores. However, IQ testing is heavily based in linguistic and logical/mathematical aptitudes, while potentially overlooking other abilities (Colangelo & Davis, 1997). Although not often recognized, young children with multiple exceptionalities (such as children with both autism and cerebral palsy) can also be gifted or talented. According to Willard-Holt (1999), gifted students with disabling conditions are least likely to receive the attention needed to address and fully develop their gifts and talents, and that in turn fails to maximize their learning and developmental outcomes. Consider the following example of a 2nd-grader with an individualized education program (IEP):

> One child who struggles academically . . . I would never know how smart he really is if it weren't for ramps! He talks about it all the

time. His reading shot up—his reading fluency has gone up. Kids are experiencing success in school because of ramps! (2nd-grade teacher, personal communication, January 22, 2009)

Teachers can easily underestimate children's learning potential and aptitude when children struggle academically (whether or not they have a disability). Creative activities like R&P allow children to demonstrate their potential learning aptitude, interests, and talents. Improved teacher expectations, combined with increased learner motivation during R&P activities, translates into overall improved academic performance across academic areas. R&P results in heightened learning experiences for teachers and children alike.

Our stance is that giftedness is much more than IQ points or grades, and can be viewed in diverse ways. R&P provides all learners with opportunities to (1) construct practical physical science concepts and relationships about force and motion, (2) explore and communicate observations made during R&P activities, (3) plan and conduct simple investigations, and (4) identify and change/adjust variables in order to solve problems while engineering and executing ramp structures. As children increase their knowledge and understanding while building ramp structures, their structures become increasingly complex (see Photos 5.1 and 5.2).

In addition to enhancing learners' scientific thinking, R&P activities help to (1) develop acceptance of errors as an integral part of the learning process (which is particularly helpful to children who are easily frustrated or have perfectionist tendencies); (2) allow for multiple means of expressing what is learned (including writings, drawings, and oral demonstrations); and (3) build social skills and acceptance of peers with differing abilities.

Students who are considered gifted and talented are not negatively stigmatized as intellectually inferior, as can happen to children with disabilities or DLLs. For this reason, Alderman (2008) insists that these learners can easily be overlooked within diverse learning communities, thus failing to maximize their fullest potential as well. When our focus includes learners considered the most able, however, our overall expectations and subsequent outcomes increase across *all* learners within diverse settings.

Learners with high science aptitudes frequently possess varied interests, hobbies, and experiences from which to draw insights and perspectives (Clark, 2002). Learners who are self-starters, as described below, enjoy building and releasing objects on ramp structures.

Students are 100% engaged! My "builder" started going in different directions—others observed his ideas! Thinking innovatively, making relationships about marble sizes and slopes, using shelves as a ladder system, problem solving with PVC piping, and using curved blocks to turn corners. Asking questions and explaining structures! Great cooperating and collaborating! (K–2 teacher, personal communication, January 22, 2009)

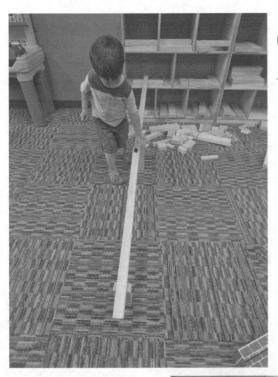

Photo 5.1. A Child Builds a Ramp Structure with One Slope

Photo 5.2. A Child Builds a Multi-tiered Ramp Structure within a Confined Space

All learners prosper in diverse settings. Children's inspirations as they build ramps can further stimulate and inspire their peers' interest and participation.

Children Identified as Dual-Language Learners (DLLs)

Children who are DLLs range in their ability to communicate in English either orally or in writing but do not demonstrate delays in their native language. To support language development, children must be provided with meaningful opportunities to explore their physical and social (cultural) environments and to communicate about their experiences with peers, caregivers, and significant adults. Science instruction with children who are identified as DLLs needs to specifically capitalize on self-confidence and cultural identity in order to increase children's willingness to converse with peers and adults (Fradd & Lee, 1995; Fredericks & Cheesebrough, 1998).

Children identified as DLLs, like all learners, can prosper from the same opportunities to develop scientific thinking and social skills offered to children considered gifted and talented. The hands-on, three-dimensional nature of building structures with wooden ramps stimulates and appeals to learners' visual-spatial, tactile, and kinesthetic learning modalities that are foundational to young children's learning experiences.

R&P creates an open, flexible social atmosphere that immerses young children in the English language. This language-rich atmosphere is beneficial to many different groups of children: children who are DLLs; children considered gifted and talented; children with speech, language, and communication delays and disabilities; and children who are extremely shy and introverted.

Children hear vocabulary and grammar (parts of speech) used in context in real time as they actively interact with ramp experts (adults and advanced peers) who use advanced vocabulary that includes various nouns, verbs, adjectives, and adverbs used to describe what is happening. Language-rich discussions during R&P experiences encourage children to expand on their expressive and receptive vocabulary, meaning, and word usage as they engage with the ramps and materials (see Figure 5.1).

Figure 5.1. Expanding Children's Vocabulary

MARBLES		
Nouns	Adjectives	Verbs
Ball	Round	Roll
Sphere	Circular	Spiral
	Spherical	Rotate
		Spin

As children's confidence in their ramp building increases, their determination to communicate their ideas and experiences with others also increases. Children are eager to share what they learn (such as explaining different strategies used to make the marble change direction) using whatever means of communication is available to them (see Photo 5.3). Children with limited expressive language skills can access other methods of communication at their disposal, such as pointing, gesturing, and motioning to peers and adults as their verbal English language skills (vocabulary and usage) gradually emerge.

Connecting language to literacy can also be achieved through children's documentation of their R&P experiences. One classroom teacher used R&P as part of her written language curriculum. Giving students an opportunity to write about what they know or have discovered increases their confidence in sharing their ideas.

DLLs and other emergent readers can benefit from opportunities to connect science learning with early literacy skills. Labeling parts of the classroom and R&P materials (for example, blocks, ramps, marbles, buckets) with English and Spanish names enriches the language experience

Photo 5.3. Child Points to Ramp Sections to Help Explain His Structure

for all learners. Identifying, describing, and explaining ramp structures using visual organizers like semantic maps can enhance early literacy skills (word recognition, vocabulary usage, and comprehension). Children can write or dictate stories or expository writings explaining how to build their ramps step-by-step with drawings or illustrations. Children can draw diagrams of their ramp structures or use photo images, identifying and labeling the different structural features (such as slope, incline, corner, tunnel, arch, or fulcrum).

When young children figure out how to build a ramp structure so that the marble will move in a desired (or sometimes unexpected) way, the experience compels children to want to share their new experience with adults and peers. According to one early childhood special education (ECSE) teacher:

> There is a language explosion for kids with speech and language deficits as they work with science relationships! They now ask each other what their ramps do! (ECSE teacher, personal communication, January 22, 2009)

Paying particular attention to children's cultural backgrounds and experiences can be especially important for young children whose culture is different from the dominant culture, such as children who are DLLs. Understanding, valuing, appreciating, and celebrating cultural differences helps build children's confidence and willingness to converse with peers and adults (Fredericks & Cheesebrough, 1998; Victor, Kellough, & Tai, 2008). Connecting children's ramp structures to real-life examples in their communities (for example, playground slides, bike ramps, and handicapped entrance ramps) helps children think about practical implications of inclines, energy, force, and motion.

Children Identified with Disabilities

No group of children is more varied, broad, or diverse than the subgroup containing children with disabilities. For children 3 to 8 years, this group generally includes children with developmental delays in one or more of the developmental areas (cognitive, communication, social, emotional, or adaptive domains). The diversity and extreme differences across disabilities (such as Down syndrome, blindness, autism, cerebral palsy), the complexity of what happens when children have multiple disabilities (such as having a hearing impairment combined with Down syndrome), and what each means in terms of development, learning, and appropriate instructional practice make general recommendations difficult and warrant caution to refrain from making overgeneralizations.

Rather than operate according to biased assumptions based on categories, teachers should focus on each learner's composite learning profile to guide and inform instructional practice and intervention. R&P, like all activities-oriented science programs, capitalizes on science learning as a dynamic process of exploration and discovery that lends itself to individual learning profiles. Activities and real materials (such as wooden ramps, blocks, and different-sized marbles) are emphasized and reading and writing skills are used to record, communicate, and support scientific learning and thinking (as described and elaborated in Chapters 2 and 4).

Deciding which strategies and approaches will most effectively entice young children with disabilities to engage in R&P activities will depend largely on the nature and extent of the individual child's strengths and limitations, impairments, medical conditions, and type of disability(s). Initial engagement may require a more direct approach involving an adult or mediated peer who builds ramp structures and invites the child with limited prior knowledge, understanding, experience, or disabilities to join the activity.

Additional Considerations Across Diverse Learners

Not all young children have had equal opportunities or access to building with blocks (wooden, cardboard, plastic, interlocking, and so on). Some children may not have access to building materials in their home. Building with blocks may not be a familiar play activity among children representing different cultures (such as Native Americans). Teacher, caregiver, and parent assumptions concerning children's interests, abilities, and talents may result in adults failing to encourage young children to play and build with blocks. Determining children's interest and prior knowledge or experience with building structures is an important first step before introducing R&P to young children.

Children who are shy, apprehensive, reluctant to take risks, have tactile defensiveness, or who require additional time to orient themselves spatially and physically with ramp materials because of sensory impairments such as blindness would further benefit greatly from extensive and repeated opportunities to work with R&P materials. Children's frequent, repeated exposure to ramp materials and where they are stored helps level the playing field by increasing children's familiarity and the comfort level they need to readily find, access, and use the materials with their peers.

Careful observation reveals which items and arrangements different children gravitate toward and actively engage in, such as whether children prefer to work alone, with a buddy, or in a small group. One preschooler with severe language delays was so excited and inspired by R&P, his mother reported that her son lined up firewood logs at home and tried to make his rubber ball roll along the length of the logs. After the ECSE preschool teacher explained to the mother that her son was trying to replicate making ramp pathways like the ones he had built at school, his mother exclaimed, "How can I purchase a set for my son to use at home?" (ECSE teacher, personal communication, December 4, 2008).

When R&P is first introduced at circle time (as described in Chapter 2), children who are less self-confident to voice their ideas publicly during problem-solving discussions may want to write, draw, or verbalize their ideas into a tape recorder. Children's ideas can then be shared and discussed once all learners are afforded adequate time to process and construct possible solutions.

CREATING EARLY SCIENCE OPPORTUNITIES
FOR DIVERSE LEARNERS

As emphasized by the ITM, observation is the single most encompassing activity teachers can use to determine the extent to which learners are interested in materials and engaged in R&P activities (see Photo 5.4). Information and insights gained through teacher observations are then used to guide, inform, and make instructional decisions using R&P.

Patterns and trends in young children's learning and development during R&P activities reveal whether children are progressing as expected across the different developmental domains or whether there are potential delays that require further assessment and intervention.

The following evidence-based practices proven beneficial to the full range of learners are recommended to support teaching practice and maximize learner outcomes during R&P activities. R&P's universal design for learning liberates teachers to use any accommodation, modification, or intervention that is needed in any context, at any given time, with any individual learner.

Maximizing Opportunity Begins with ZPD and Scaffolding

Learning for all children begins at the zone of proximal development (ZPD). Vygotsky's (1935/1978) best-known concept, ZPD is conceptualized as the space between what a child can do by him- or herself and what the child is capable of doing with support. During R&P activities, teachers must carefully observe children to determine the extent to which the child can independently build a ramp structure, the complexity of the structure, and when, how, and the extent to which the teacher can assist or intervene to challenge the child's understanding and skill development.

Teachers can easily scaffold (assist) children's learning as the child completes R&P activities as independently as possible. Productive questioning, as described in Chapters 2 and 4, is one form of assistance that teachers use to scaffold young children's thinking and understanding. However, it is important to keep scaffolding to a minimum in order to avoid interfering with the child's agenda (what he or she wants to make happen) and problem solving.

Photo 5.4. Teacher Observes and Documents the Child's Ramp Structure

For example, a preschool boy with cognitive delays wanted a marble to pass through a hole in a block. He placed the block with the hole positioned facedown on the floor. When he released the marble, he watched it skid across the block without passing through the hole. He would shift the block, but always kept it flat on the floor (ECSE teacher, personal communication, October 30, 2008).

The ECSE teachers' repeated observations revealed that the preschooler had not yet developed the spatial reasoning needed to accurately determine how to position the block in order to make the marble roll through the hole. According to this child's ZPD, the teacher could expand on his experiences by introducing other materials, such as plastic rings with larger openings and paper towel tubes, and challenge the child to make the marble roll through the openings.

Most of the time, students who have prior experiences with R&P materials have an agenda of their own—something they want to try to figure out. In contrast, students with diverse learning needs may struggle with creating their own agenda. They may need guidance getting started, or they may try the same repetitive structure over and over again because they were successful at constructing it. Scaffolded assistance can take many different variations, depending on children's diverse needs (for example, physical assistance such as hand-under-hand) (see Photo 5.5).

Photo 5.5. Teacher Helps the Child with Block Placement Using a Hand-Under-Hand Approach

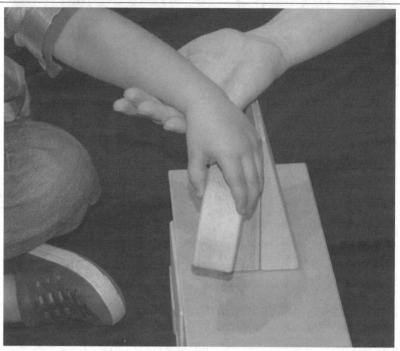

Scaffolded assistance is intentionally reduced as the child's skill development and understanding increases (Berk & Winsler, 1995; Kame'enui, Carnine, Dixon, Simmons, & Coyne, 2002). Productive questioning, on the other hand, is not reduced or eliminated, but rather is an integral means of guiding and facilitating the inquiry process.

When learners get "stuck" on repetitive building (repeatedly building the same structure time after time), it is important to move children along in their development by providing additional prompts and challenges to learn new skills. The student may have developed a nicely functioning ramp, and may be afraid to make changes that might lead to the ramp no longer working. Encouraging the student to add two or three pieces may be enough to get him or her to think of different ideas.

Peer Mediators Invite Engagement and Social Participation

Utilizing advanced peers as mediators or peer supports is a natural, non-intrusive way to promote young children's active participation during R&P activities. Peer mediation, like science mentorship for teachers, is an exclusively social activity (Counsell, 2011). Peer mediators can model, encourage, and support others' efforts and understanding as they attempt to build ramp structures.

For learners who are discouraged, or who have a limited knowledge base, teachers can set up a simple ramp. They can guide the student in making minor adjustments to tweak the structure so that the student can experience success. Carefully selecting and pairing the student with a preferred peer (peer mediator) may help increase involvement and interest in R&P activities.

Peer or teacher mediation during additional block time may be an opportunity for the student to gain additional assistance in working on a structure that he or she is struggling with.

The teacher can provide the peer mediator with guidance on how to communicate and encourage active participation, and on which behaviors to avoid (see Figure 5.2). R&P activities are naturally conducive to group-work, allowing expert ramp builders to spontaneously serve as peer mediators, as suggested by this 2nd-grade teacher:

> I have little engineers in my class. They run around and help others to problem-solve! (2nd-grade teacher, personal communication, May 7, 2009)

Peer mediation can lead to, and support, spontaneous group-work. A learning atmosphere that promotes safe, accepting, and supportive collaboration encourages expert builders to spontaneously support less advanced, novice ramp builders, achieving common goals as they build ramp structures. Working together enables *all* learners to exchange (and accept) differing ideas and points of view, share materials, and work toward a common goal. Reciprocal relationships often result when the peer mediator who has advanced skills during ramp building may become the child receiving assistance in another context, such as drawing. The assisted peer who has advanced skills in drawing now becomes the peer mediator in this context.

Figure 5.2. Peer Mediator Strategies

Communication	Active Engagement	Behaviors to Avoid
Sign language	Handling blocks or ramps	Directing ramp building
Asking questions/ probing	Retrieving materials	Telling/imposing ramp solutions
Prompting	Sharing materials and space	Competing to be the best
Constructive feedback	Brainstorming possible solutions through trial and error	Judging or criticizing others' efforts

Teachers consistently report that children are eager and excited to work together during R&P activities. As one explained:

> Four children made two jumps at the same time. So exciting, so happy—had a mutual idea and did it together. (ECSE teacher, personal communication, October 30, 2008)

Children explode with enthusiasm when they unite and accomplish shared goals. Learning and development for any child (with or without disabilities) is maximized when children are assured access to social learning contexts (Counsell, 2009). The more children work cooperatively together, the more they develop a sense of community.

Building Community Membership Instills Acceptance

Peer supports and collaborative group practices help develop and sustain a learning environment in which all children are valued as members of the learning community. According to Kliewer (1998), "One does not learn membership apart from being a member" (p. 317). R&P activities are completed within a social context in which no child is excluded and every child is viewed as a valuable member of the community. As one teacher explained:

> I have several students with special needs. You wouldn't know who they are as they talk about their ramps—very excited about what they are doing. With R&P, all children work together at different levels of understanding. (Kindergarten teacher, personal communication, March 19, 2009)

Social activities that value all members' participation and contributions foster and support children's complex cognition and learning (Siegel, 2001). This in turn increases children's acceptance of multiple perspectives and contributes to interactions that are cooperative rather than competitive in nature.

When children work together, they learn how to share materials, negotiate, and compromise with peers. The learning opportunities during group activities are greater than the children would otherwise experience if they constructed and executed ramp structures alone. Children learn to see others as valued members of a group (whether it be the marble releaser, the corner expert, the detective who locates where the marble exited, or the structural maintenance patrol, to name a few). For example, one teacher described a "marble keeper" as follows:

> I have one child who has an IEP who is so excited about the marbles. He wanted to be in charge of the marbles. We created an inventory

for the marbles and it became his job to be in charge. He counts the marbles and checks the list every day! He is improving his counting skills, which happens to be a math goal on his IEP. (2nd-grade teacher, personal communication, September 4, 2008)

Augmentative and Alternative Communication Empowers Social Interaction

Augmentative and alternative communication (AAC) is an important form of assistive technology used to increase young children's access to socialization, learning, and daily routines. Assistive technology refers to any device, piece of equipment, or product system—whether acquired commercially, modified, or customized—that is used to aid, increase, maintain, or improve the functional capabilities of children with disabilities.

AAC devices enhance and expand upon children's existing communication skills and behaviors. They make it possible for children who have no speech or other means of communication to communicate (Cook, Klein, & Tessier, 2008). Though many AAC systems involve electronic and computer-assisted technology, many low-tech systems and activities can be readily used to support children's engagement.

A digital camera and printer are invaluable tools in designing AAC systems for children who do not have functional oral language. Teachers may find it helpful to include photos illustrating R&P items, concepts, and relationships such as ramp pieces (showing four different sizes), supports (blocks, boxes, sponges, furniture), and objects (balls, marbles, cubes, spools, beads, micro-cars).

Children can communicate with peers and adults during R&P activities by pointing to pictures or taking pictures from a book, binder, or chart and giving the pictures to peers or adults. Interaction should not be limited to children only making requests for items that they want or need. Children should

---

AUGMENTATIVE AND ALTERNATIVE COMMUNICATION

Teachers can use an assortment of AAC devices to support children's communication during R&P activities. A sampling of affordable, low-tech solutions include the following:

- Manual sign language
- Color photos on a communication board
- Color photos in a communication book
- Picture exchange communication system (PECS)
- Letter and word cards

also be encouraged to combine sequences of pictures to communicate phrases and sentences (for instance, "The big red block is placed under the longest ramp") and illustrate in a drawing. Children can also be taught how to use a digital camera and photos to tell a story (as elaborated upon in Chapter 6).

The same words, concepts, and relationships can be recorded using complex, multilevel electronic communication devices such as BIGmack (Ablenet), TalkPad (Frame Technologies), Cheap Talk (Enabling Devices), and Tango!™ (Dynavox). Letter and word keyboards can be used as children develop literacy skills, science concepts, and vocabulary.

ACCOMMODATING DEVELOPMENTAL CONSIDERATIONS DURING SCIENCE ACTIVITIES

In addition to science inquiry, scientific knowledge, and design, R&P activities also provide opportunities for learning and skill development across multiple developmental domains and content areas. Teachers can easily create short teaching episodes (mini-lessons) and learning skills instruction, embedding learning objectives identified on young children's individualized family service plans (IFSPs), individualized education programs (IEPs), or intervention plans for DLLs directly into R&P activities. The following discussions outline possible accommodations to address a range of learning and developmental considerations across developmental domains during R&P activities.

Accommodating Cognitive Considerations

Children experiencing cognitive delays or learning challenges often have difficulties with cognitive processing, memory, or problem-solving skills that are key to science learning. R&P materials and activities are very beneficial to young children with cognitive considerations. To accommodate learners, teachers can:

- provide additional cues such as gestures (for example, pointing to where the marble exited the ramp) or picture cues of ramp materials;
- observe the targeted child build ramp structures with peers and use descriptive talk or think-alouds to help the child think about (process) what the children are doing. The think-aloud strategy helps children think through the process by saying out loud what is required to successfully complete a specific task; and
- use competent ramp builders as peer supports to help describe and explain their ramp structures.

Accommodating Language and Communication Considerations

At the preschool level, young children qualify for language-related services more than any other developmental domain. Important communication skills for young children to master include speaking clearly, communicating wants and needs, understanding others' wants and needs, and conversing reciprocally with peers and adults. Open-ended questions used to guide and facilitate children's scientific thinking and learning encourage children to respond beyond simple yes/no answers. These are particularly challenging to young children with communication considerations. To further support children's communication, teachers can:

- learn, use, and prepare children's AAC system regularly (as described earlier) during R&P activities;
- position themselves face-to-face during all communications and model this strategy for peer supports as well; and
- expand upon children's expressive language by commenting or repeating children's statements with additional vocabulary and information.

Teachers and speech language pathologists can work together to create situations designed to address speech fluency, vocabulary development, and articulation goals. For example, an embedded learning opportunity (ELO) could be to work with a student on the /sl/ blend during R&P such as *slope*, *slide*, and *slip*. Word meaning and usage are reinforced and expanded as the child applies and generalizes *slope*, *slide*, and *slip* to different activities, routines, and events in different settings (at school and home) throughout the child's day (for example, during outdoor play on the playground slide).

Accommodating Fine and Gross Motor Considerations

Children experiencing fine or gross motor delays may have differences in their ability to use joints, bones, or muscles because of contributing medical conditions such as cerebral palsy, spina bifida, or muscular dystrophy. Unique abilities and movement patterns warrant the need to consult physical or occupational therapists for specialized support services and appropriate use of adaptive equipment. To accommodate fine and gross motor considerations, teachers can:

- provide ample time and physical space for children to get R&P materials and move around as they build ramp structures;
- use Rubbermaid shelving liner, Velcro, or other nonslip material to help stabilize ramps and wooden blocks;

- use large cardboard blocks or sponges that children can easily grasp;
- use hula-hoops, colored tape, or tabletops to establish and maintain a workspace and field of vision;
- provide children with mobility items such as a toy shopping cart to explore and transport ramp materials;
- use adaptive positioning items to support children's posture (stabilized and supported trunk) and free the child's hands to reach, hold, or handle R&P materials; and
- use correctly sized adapted chairs to allow the child's feet to rest flat on the floor or on an elevated footrest.

Fine motor development is encouraged as children build, make careful adjustments, and fine-tune their ramp structures in order to achieve desired outcomes (for instance, the marble turns a corner). Picking up, holding, and releasing marbles facilitate fine motor development and reinforce the child's development of the "pincer grip" (an important fine motor skill used during handwriting). Occupational therapists can provide additional support as children engage with R&P materials.

R&P is not outside the capabilities of students with ambulatory needs (students who use gait trainers, walkers, crutches, or wheelchairs). Tabletop structures can provide safe work areas and stability for children to lean up against or walk around without the use of physical aids (see Photo 5.6).

Tables can also increase both access and independence during ramp building for a child who uses a wheelchair by allowing the child to move around the structure and observe the ramps from a variety of angles.

ADAPTIVE POSITIONING EQUIPMENT USED BY SPECIAL EDUCATORS AND OCCUPATIONAL THERAPISTS

The following furniture items (tables and chairs) help to support children's sitting posture as they build ramp structures.

- Sling seats
- Boppys
- E-Z Lyers
- Wedges
- Floor tables
- Corner seats
- Sassy seats
- Rifton chairs
- Exersaucers

Photo 5.6. Children Build Ramp Slopes on the Tabletop

Accommodating Social and Emotional Considerations

Children who have temperaments that are inflexible, intolerant, or easily agitated can experience social rejection from peers that further impedes or hinders their social (and communication) development. R&P capitalizes on cooperative learning that promotes important social skills as children build ramp structures together.

R&P PROMOTES SOCIAL SKILLS

Ramp Building in Groups Allows for

- Invitations to participate
- Initiating conversations
- Deciding what happens
- Asking and answering questions
- Taking turns
- Sharing items

These social skills further enable children who may struggle with maintaining positive peer relationships to participate in a wide range of additional activities and experiences (such as developing meaningful friendships).

To further promote social skills during R&P activities, teachers can:

- create an inviting, warm, noncompetitive learning atmosphere;
- encourage children to help formulate simple rules outlining basic conduct when using R&P (as described in Chapters 2 and 4);
- maintain a regular routine/schedule for children to work with R&P in order to ensure children's sense of security;
- create varied workspaces that allow for small groups to build ramp structures cooperatively and quiet workspaces that allow children to build ramp structures independently; and
- use peer supports to help model appropriate social behaviors (quiet indoor voice, using words to express wants, needs, and emotions, or the proper way to carry ramps).

One teacher had two male students with behavior plans who struggled socially in her class. When these two students participated in R&P, she said:

I have two boys with behavior plans in my class. Building with ramps helps them with managing and coping! Learning to cooperate, get along, and work together is crucial to children who struggle. Cooperative learning is instilled. (2nd-grade teacher, personal communication, November 13, 2008)

Accommodating Hearing and Visual Considerations

Learning is a social activity in which much of the knowledge conveyed to learners is done orally, relying heavily on learners' auditory processing, receptive language (comprehension), and hearing ability. Hearing loss can range from mild losses to profound deafness. Specialists such as audiologists, speech and language pathologists, and deaf educators provide the necessary services to assess, recommend treatment, and help develop communication strategies and approaches. To accommodate learners' hearing considerations, teachers can do the following:

- Familiarize yourself with the use, storage, and maintenance of adaptive aids (such as hearing aids).
- Emphasize the importance and necessity of the child's adaptive aids to the child's peers.
- Learn and use the child's AAC system (such as sign language).
- Post information about the AAC system (such as American Sign Language illustrations around the block area) as a reference for peers and adults.

- Monitor excess noise and potential auditory distractions during ramp-building activities, as hearing aids amplify all environmental sounds.
- Always speak face-to-face when communicating and ascertain the child's attention visually before asking questions, making comments, or beginning a new activity.
- Model effective communication strategies with peer supports.
- Speak clearly and concisely, using gestures to emphasize key words or ideas. Repeat or rephrase as necessary to ensure the child's understanding.
- Use visual cues such as pictures, printed words, or ramp materials to help support and convey meaning.
- Check frequently for understanding throughout the inquiry process.

R&P is also a visual, spatially oriented physical science activity. For this reason, creating ways to guarantee that children with visual limitations can participate in R&P activities may pose the greatest challenge to early childhood educators. Visual considerations can range from partial vision to complete blindness. Vision specialists (along with orientation and mobility specialists) provide important services designed to help children utilize what vision they have in order to be as independent as possible. Recommendations include the following:

- Help the child become oriented to the classroom layout at the beginning of the school year and maintain ample floor space in the ramp center for R&P activities.
- Learn what the child can see and how to position objects so that the child can see them most easily.
- Use high-contrast colors with building materials (such as large cardboard blocks or sponges) with colors such as black and yellow together.
- Encourage children with prescription eyeglasses to consistently wear them.
- Maximize lighting conditions according to the child's needs.
- Keep pathways clear to designated area(s) for ramp building.
- Always use the child's name when initiating communication.
- Use specific directional language during ramp building and help the child to physically feel the spatial orientation with his or her hands as you speak.
- Use auditory cues such as cat toy balls with bells that the child can hear and track through the auditory channel as the balls move along the pathways.
- Use tactile cues such as Rubbermaid liners to help denote the ends of ramps.

DIRECTIONAL LANGUAGE WITH
CHILDREN WHO ARE VISUALLY IMPAIRED

Children with visual challenges generally rely on their auditory skills to help compensate for their visual limitations. Using clear, concise, and accurate directional terms during R&P activities helps a child with visual challenges to follow the trajectory of a moving object (such as a marble) that is released on a ramp structure.

- Over, Under, Beneath, Below
- Beside, Next to
- In Front, Behind

CONCLUSION

The purpose of this chapter is to illustrate that *all children are science learners* as they engage in high-quality, universally designed early science activities such as R&P. Although we discuss and provide helpful recommendations for maximizing learning and development outcomes through R&P activities with children identified as gifted and talented, dual-language learners (DLLs), or having disabilities, we continually warn against the pitfalls of sorting children categorically. Instead, our emphasis is first and foremost to recognize and satisfy each child's individual uniqueness along the continuum of learning and development. To achieve this goal, we assert that *all* children must be guaranteed universal access to, and participation in, science activities like R&P.

This chapter illustrates the compatibility between the Inquiry Teaching Model (ITM) and universally designed learning (UDL). The ITM's flexibility easily allows for (1) accommodations, modifications, and interventions; (2) zone of proximal development (ZPD) and scaffolding; (3) peer mediators; (4) community membership; and (5) augmentative and alternative communication (AAC) during R&P activities. General accommodations used during R&P to foster and maximize diverse learners' skill acquisition, learning, and development across different developmental domains and academic content areas are outlined.

Always keep in mind that no two children are identical learners. Outcomes will invariably be different because learners are undeniably different. R&P activities cannot guarantee that all children will achieve identical outcomes in terms of learning and development in general and gains in scientific thinking and understanding specifically.

Learners do not share the same aptitudes or interests in science. A continuum of learning and development among any group of diverse learners will likewise translate into a continuum of science outcomes and achievement. An emphasis on what is educationally relevant and personally respectful to young children along a continuum of development can increase the likelihood that individual achievement will be maximized using R&P. This makes R&P a win-win learning experience for *all* learners and educators alike.

CHAPTER 6

Ramps and Pathways and STEM + Literacy

Beth Van Meeteren

In Chapter 4, we showcased how Ramps and Pathways (R&P) investigations are fertile ground for literacy and social development as children strive to communicate to solve problems and share successes. In this chapter, we explore how R&P neatly fits within recent recommendations for science, technology, and engineering education (National Research Council, 2012) in the kindergarten and primary classroom. We provide a sound argument to anyone who questions the educational rigor and value of R&P in an early childhood classroom and illustrate how the chapter's author was able to integrate R&P investigations in the literacy block in her 1st-grade classroom. Once in place, R&P not only addressed standards within the *Next Generation Science Standards* (NGSS) but also standards within the *Common Core State Standards for English Language Arts & Literacy* and the *Common Core State Standards for Mathematics* (National Governors Association Center for Best Practices & Council of Chief State School Officers, 2010a, 2010b).

A PLACE FOR STEM IN THE KINDERGARTEN AND PRIMARY CLASSROOM

The NGSS challenge schools and teachers to create educational environments that will allow children to engage in the practices of science and engineering (NRC, 2013). Many administrators and primary teachers may feel STEM is too difficult for young students and believe instructional efforts and time should focus on the development of literacy and mathematics in the primary grades, leaving the challenges of STEM to upper elementary. They are mistaken. The authors of the National Research Council's *Taking Science to School* (2007) warned that science education has not fully valued the cognitive abilities of young children and they encouraged teachers to engage kindergarten and primary grade children in more rigorous work in science explorations. When closely observing their young students outside the formal classroom, administrators and teachers learn that children are already engaging in STEM on their own. Young children independently explore the physical world to figure out how they can control it on a nearly continuous basis (Kato & Van Meeteren, 2008). One only needs to watch children on a playground to see this in action. For example, children sitting in a swing find they can move with a push or a pull by another child or an adult. By systematically shifting their body weight on the swing, they figure out how to get the swing to move without anyone else's help. When they cease to shift their weight, the swing eventually slows to a stop. By dragging their feet on the ground, they hasten the stop. In effect, children engineer their actions as well as innovate on the original design of the swing. (Who hasn't been irritated by having to unwind the chains of a swing thrown around the top by previous riders who wanted to figure out how shorter chains affect the action of the swing?) Children develop a relational understanding of how subtle variations of their actions, or a redesign (engineering of technology), affect the movement of the swing (physical science). They observe and measure the action of the swing through the lens of spatial thinking (mathematics) as they note the height and arch of the swing's movement and count the number of passes the swing makes until it finally stops. In short, children interact with the universe (engineering and technology) in order to understand and explain the universe (science and mathematics). This is when STEM is relevant to the young child. Schools only need to conceptualize what developing science and engineering behaviors look like, and do a bit of rearranging within the current classroom settings, and these schools will allow STEM to flourish within the formal classroom from the very start of a child's education. At the same time, they will notice a plethora of opportunities to entice children to learn the tools of literacy.

Standards Within Ramps and Pathways

When developing the new standards that guide the revision of science curriculum, its implementation, and assessment, the National Research Council (2012) recommended that the standards be developed around three dimensions:

- Crosscutting concepts that unify the study of science and engineering
- Scientific and engineering practices
- Core ideas in four disciplinary areas: physical sciences; life sciences; earth and space sciences; and engineering, technology, and the applications of science

To facilitate learning, the NRC recommended that the dimensions should be woven together in standards, curricula, instruction, and assessments. For example, when exploring the forces and motion core idea —How can one predict an object's continued motion, changes in motion, or stability? (National Research Council, 2012)—children should be fully engaged in the practices of science and engineering. They should be allowed the time, materials, and freedom to construct a developing understanding of this core idea and to develop as independent learners. Teachers can guide children to associate the crosscutting concepts to help them construct an understanding of how everything is connected (NRC, 2012).

R&P fits the vision of the NGSS in kindergarten, 1st, and 2nd grades like a glove. R&P addresses physical science disciplinary core ideas and engineering design core ideas (as described in Chapter 1) in kindergarten through 2nd grade (NRC, 2013). Throughout R&P investigations, children are heavily engaged in science and engineering practices as they plan and carry out investigations, and analyze and interpret data. In the process, they find themselves engaging with concepts that cut across the domains such as cause and effect, patterns, systems and system models, structure and function, and most of all, the interdependence of science, engineering, and technology. R&P explorations are a powerful example of how kindergarten and primary grade teachers can implement a fully integrated STEM curriculum within the NGSS guidelines. This may be best illustrated by a sampling of R&P challenges. In the following section, the context for an R&P challenge is provided along with a list of materials, a careful consideration of the variables within the investigation that will influence conceptual development, suggestions for introducing each activity, and suggestions for questions and comments to support children in their developmental practice of science and engineering. We caution that the list is not exhaustive, nor is it a strict linear progression of challenges. These samplings are not intended to be used in a rigid sequential or hierarchical sense, but as a framework from which to begin.

A SAMPLING OF RAMP ACTIVITY CHALLENGES

BUILDING ONE-PIECE RAMPS: VARIOUS HEIGHTS
(A GOOD BEGINNING FOR ALL AGES)

After children have had ample opportunity and time to build with unit blocks, they gain enough understanding about weight, balance, friction, tension, and stability to allow them to take on the challenge of creating ramp and pathway systems. It is best to limit the amount and kinds of materials at the beginning to support children's development of the fundamental relationships necessary in building ramps and pathways. In this exploration, materials are limited to allow children to develop relationships between the height of a ramp and the action of a marble. This can be introduced to a large or small group of children.

Materials:

- Short pieces of cove molding (track)
- Dry sponges or unit blocks for supports
- Spheres of the same size and weight (with 3-year-olds, use larger marbles to ensure safety if children still mouth objects)

Things that children can vary or change:

- Heights of ramps
- Number of track segments
- The position of the unit blocks in creating the supports

Design constraints or things for the teacher to hold constant or the same:

- Everyone gets the same length of cove molding or track
- Everyone gets the same type of sphere

Relationships children have the possibility of making:

- Between the high end of the ramp and the direction of the marble
- Between the height of the ramp and the speed of the marble
- Between the spot the marble is released on the first ramp section and the speed of the marble (the farther up on the ramp, the faster it rolls)
- Between the height of the ramp and the force with which it hits another object placed at the end of the ramp
- Between the height of the ramp and the distance traveled by the marble off the ramp

Examples of a teacher's introduction:

> *I noticed you have built some interesting and stable block structures. I'm going to add these pieces of track to the block center along with some marbles. I'm wondering what you can do with the blocks and tracks to make the marble move on the track.*

> *I'm adding some track to the block center.* [Lay a track flat on the floor and place a marble in the middle.] *What do you suppose we could do to move the marble from here* [pointing to the marble in the middle] *to there* [pointing to the space off the end of the track]?

[Allow the children to suggest and try out their ideas.] *I'm going to leave these materials in the center so you can continue to explore what you can do.*

Examples of questions and comments to inspire reasoning:

Is there a way you can get the marble to go in another direction?

What could you do to make the marble stop about here? [Point to a spot on the table.]

What could you do to make the marble go past here? [Point to a spot on the table.]

Is there a way you could get the marble to knock down this block when it comes off the ramp?

I notice the marble went farther that time. What did you do to make that happen?

BUILDING ONE-PIECE RAMPS: VARIOUS OBJECTS
(A GOOD BEGINNING FOR ALL AGES)

After children have had ample opportunity and time to build and vary the height using one-piece ramps, they can build one-piece ramps and release various objects in order to observe what happens with each object. A gradual introduction of different materials allows children to construct mental relationships between the properties of an object and how the properties affect the object's motion.

Materials:

- Lots of different objects of different properties (wooden spools, jingle bells, small cars, wooden cubes, dice, feathers, small pinecones, LEGOs, plastic eggs, paper clip, wheels from toys, stones, crayon, penny, clothespins, tops, spheres, popsicle sticks . . . just look in your teacher junk drawer)
- Cove molding or track
- Unit blocks

Things that children can vary or change:

- The height of the ramp
- The object placed on the track or ramp

Design constraints or things for the teacher to hold constant or the same:

- Everyone gets one piece of the same length of cove molding or track

Relationships children have the possibility of making:

- Between the properties of the object and how those properties affect movement
- Between the slope of the ramp and the ability to move each object

Example of a teacher's introduction:

> *I wonder how many of these things we can get to move on a ramp. Do you suppose they will all work for us?*

Examples of questions and comments to inspire reasoning:

> *Is there a way to get all the objects to move down a ramp?*

> *How do the things move (roll, slide, wobble, wiggle, bounce, tumble, somersault, flip-flop, cartwheel, turn, rotate, glide, skate, skid, slither, shake, tremble, quiver)?*

> *This seems to wobble and tumble down the ramp and stops while this one slides and then turns at the bottom.*

> *Why do you suppose that rolled the farthest?*

> *I wonder why these objects all slide and these objects all roll?*

> *Can you help me figure out why this won't move?*

> *I wonder why this is so hard to move?*

> *Which objects are interesting to watch?*

> *Which objects are your favorites to move? Why are they your favorite? Does everyone agree with you?*

> *Which objects are your least favorites? Why? Does everyone agree with you?*

BUILDING ONE-PIECE RAMPS: VARIOUS SPHERES
(A GOOD BEGINNING FOR ALL AGES)

Once children figure out that spheres are easiest to move and control on ramps and they begin to primarily use spheres, you can challenge them to consider how the properties of weight and size affect a sphere's movement.

Materials:

- Spheres of different weights and sizes
- Cove molding or track
- Unit blocks

Things that children can vary or change:

- Spheres of different weights
- Spheres of different sizes (you can get ball bearings the same size as common marbles, but they weigh more)

Design constraints or things for the teacher to hold constant or the same:

- Everyone gets one piece of the same length of cove molding or track
- Everyone is encouraged to use the same number of blocks to support the high end of the ramp

Relationships children have the possibility of making:

- Between the sizes of spheres and how far they roll
- Between the weights of spheres and how far they roll

Example of a teacher's introduction:

> *I've noticed that on Deondre's ramp, the different spheres he sends down do not all move the same. I wonder if we might be able to notice/observe a pattern in how each sphere moves on a ramp.*

Examples of questions and comments to inspire reasoning:

> *Did you figure out which kinds of spheres roll the farthest?*

> *What is it about this sphere that makes it go farthest?*

> *I wonder how we can figure out which sphere rolls the fastest?*

> *Which is slowest? How do you know it goes the slowest? How could you keep track?*

> *What is it about this sphere that makes it go slowest?*

> *Which goes the shortest distance? How can we keep track?*

> *What is it about this sphere that makes it go the shortest distance?*

CONNECTING RAMP SECTIONS
(A RELATIONSHIP TO BE MADE BY ALL BEGINNING BUILDERS, YOUNG AND OLD)

Sometimes children will build a ramp using only one piece of track. Teachers can introduce the challenge of using two or more pieces of track. This presents the problem of connecting each segment of track in a way that allows the marble to move smoothly from one track onto the next. Children problem-solve to eliminate gaps by moving the ends of each track close together or overlapping the ends of the track.

Materials:

- Cove molding or track of different lengths
- Spheres of the same size and weight
- Unit blocks for supports

Things that children can vary or change:

- Placement of ramps as they connect
- Height of the starter ramp

Design constraints or things for the teacher to hold constant or the same:

- Everyone gets the same kind of sphere or marble

Relationships children have the possibility of making:

- The method of overlapping the ramp sections and the passage of the marble
- The height of the starter ramp and the speed of the marble
- The speed of the marble and the ability of the marble to pass over the connection
- The height of the starter ramp and whether or not the marble will travel to the end of the last ramp section

Example of a teacher's introduction:

I'm wondering how you could use two or three pieces of track to make a marble move.

How could you get the marble to move from one track onto the next?

How long of a track can you make? Will the marble roll all the way to the end of the track?

Examples of questions and comments to inspire reasoning:

Where is the marble going off the path?

What does the marble do when it misses the next section?

Is there a way you can fix it so you can keep the marble on the pathway?

BUILDING A RAMP WITH A JUMP OR A DROP
(WHEN BUILDERS BECOME MORE CONFIDENT)

When the teacher notices a gap between two linear ramp sections, he or she may ask the child if there is a way the marble can jump across the gap (see

Photo 6.1). (Children often associate this with motorcycle jumps they have seen on television and come up with this idea on their own.)

Materials:

- Unit blocks
- Cove molding or track of different lengths
- Marbles

Things that children can vary or change:

- The distance of the gap between the two pieces of track
- The steepness of the incline

Design constraints or things for the teacher to hold constant or the same:

- At the beginning, the teacher may guide the students to use one kind of sphere until they are successful. Afterward, the teacher may offer or suggest using other sizes or weights of spheres to see if the design is still successful. This will allow children to explore the properties of objects within the context of a different design problem.

Relationships children have the possibility of making:

- Between the speed of the marble and the arc of the marble as it leaves the end of a suspended ramp
- Between the steepness of the incline and the arc of the marble as it leaves the end

Photo 6.1. A System to Allow a Marble to Jump Over Cars

- Between the ricochet of the marble dropping onto a flat track versus the ricochet of the marble dropping onto an incline

Example of a teacher's introduction:

I notice you have a gap here, but the marble makes it across. I wonder why it isn't stopping? How wide of a gap do you think you can get the marble to jump across?

Examples of questions and comments to inspire reasoning:

What is happening to the marble at the gap?

If you wanted to keep the gap, is there a way the marble could cross it and land on the next ramp section?

I see the marble crosses the gap, but then bounces off the next ramp section. Is there something you can do to that second ramp to keep the marble from bouncing off?

Can you get it to keep working if you make the gap even wider?

USING MULTIPLE PIECES OF RAMP SECTIONS WITHIN A CONFINED AREA
(EXPERIENCED BUILDERS)

Budding ramp architects and engineers may learn that they can benefit from studying other ramp designs to enhance their own designs. Sometimes it is interesting to have a formal design challenge where everyone has the same-sized space and same materials to work with (see Photo 6.2). Children and teachers will find that there is more than one way to use the space and materials, and that children are creative with what design challenges can be solved with the same materials.

Materials:

- Masking tape
- Spheres
- Unit blocks

Things that children can vary or change:

- Design of the ramp in regard to slope and the use of corners
- Placement and height of support structures

Design constraints or things for the teacher to hold constant or the same:

- On the floor, use masking tape to mark out work areas approximately 3 feet by 3 feet in size. Being careful to use identical pieces of track for every builder, place three sections of track within each work area. Choose lengths of track that will not fit within the workspace if placed end to end. This will challenge builders to build an R&P system that allows marbles to turn corners or change direction. Also place identical spheres within each work area. Provide unit blocks to build support structures.

- Everyone gets the same size and shape of work area
- Everyone uses identical pieces of cove molding or track
- Everyone uses the same type of spheres

Relationships children have the possibility of making:

- The area of the workspace and the configuration of the ramp sections to fit within the workspace
- The height of the starter ramp and its relationship to the receiving ramp
- The slope of the ramps and the marble's movement to the last section of the system
- The configuration of the pathway and whether or not the marble stays on the track

Photo 6.2. A System That Allows a Marble to Travel a Long Distance in a Small Space

- The spatial order of ramp section placement and the temporal order of the marble's movement (first the marble will go here, then here, then here)

Class meetings provide children and teachers with important opportunities to come together to discuss, construct, and compose a working draft of a research problem to solve using R&P. Teachers can ask children to help identify the constraints everyone has to work within. Let children help to tape off 3x3 areas. Children get a beginning sense of area as opposed to linear length by helping you. This is a perfect context to address conducting a formal investigation, the kind of writing that goes into setting up a formal investigation, and observing and noticing similarities and differences in design.

Example of a teacher's introduction:

I've noticed how many different ideas everyone has when they build. I'm curious to find out how many different ideas we have even when we have the same materials. Would you like to do a little research study together?

Examples of questions and comments to inspire reasoning:

How are you going to arrange the three pieces to build your ramp?

Which piece is the beginning of your system?

Which piece will come next?

Where will you start your marble?

Can you explain where you think the marble will go before you try out the ramp?

Is there another way you could put your ramp sections together and still get the marble to roll?

If it isn't fitting inside the square, is there a way you could change the shape of your ramp?

If we take a tour of what other builders are doing, could you get some new ideas?

I notice the ball keeps rolling off this piece of the ramp section. Can you watch it here and help me figure out why?

I wonder what you could do to keep the marble from stopping on this ramp section?

Why do you suppose this corner works when this one doesn't?

BUILDING RAMPS WITH HILLS
(RAMPS THAT GO DOWN THEN UP, DOWN THEN UP, DOWN THEN UP . . .)
(EXPERIENCED BUILDERS)

After reading a book such as *Wheel Away* by Dayle Ann Dodd, students may become interested in designing ramps with hills (see Photo 6.3). Or the teacher could ask, "Is there a way you can get a marble to go up a ramp?" If the students say no, marbles only roll down, the teacher may counter, "I once saw a kindergarten/1st-/2nd-grader get a marble to go up a ramp. I wonder if you can figure out how he or she did it?" That is all it takes, and they are off!

Materials:

- Ramp sections
- Spheres
- Unit blocks

Things that children can vary or change:

- The number of hills
- The heights of the hills
- The weight and size of the sphere

Photo 6.3. A System to Allow a Marble Enough Speed to Roll Over a Series of Hills

Design constraints or things for the teacher to hold constant or the same:

- It is important to stick to one kind of sphere as much as possible. When students are successful, you can challenge them to use heavier spheres, larger spheres, or spheres made of different materials to see if the sphere still successfully travels the entire pathway.

Relationships children have the possibility of making:

- The height of the starter ramp and the speed of the marble as it crests the top of the hill
- The energy lost in the impact of the marble at the bottom of the starter ramp (if the starter ramp is too steep)

Example of a teacher's introduction:

I've noticed some builders say that marbles can only go down ramps. However, I've had other builders say they have gotten marbles to go down and up ramps. What do you think? Is there a way you can build a system to get a marble to go up a ramp?

Examples of questions and comments to inspire reasoning:

How could you build a ramp with many hills?

What supports work best for you in building a hill?

Is there a way to build that support without using so many blocks?

Is there a way to make that support sturdier?

How do you know when you make the hill too high?

How do you know when you make the hill too low?

BUILDING WITHIN AN IRREGULARLY SHAPED, CONFINED AREA
(EXPERIENCED BUILDERS)

The book *Roberto: The Insect Architect* by Nina Laden may inspire discussions about what architects do and what kinds of challenges they face. Professional architects don't get to make all the decisions when building. They have to use what they are given and have to listen to the person who is paying for the building. Teachers can ask their students if they would like to experience a little of what that might be like and invite them to complete a design task. An example may be directing students to build an R&P structure using a specific number and length of track within an oddly configured space of "real estate" (see Photo 6.4). After blocking out an area of "real estate" on the floor with masking tape,

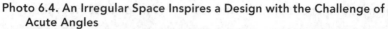

Photo 6.4. An Irregular Space Inspires a Design with the Challenge of Acute Angles

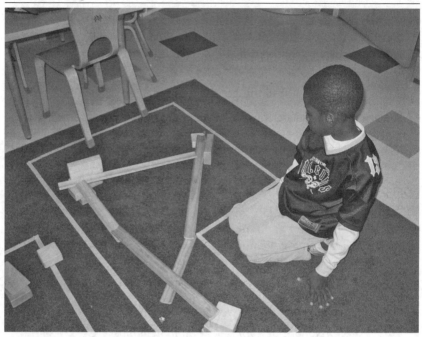

students can be challenged to build a ramp using all the sections given by the teacher within this limited space. To create a need for students to reason about corners, the teacher should choose lengths of track that when combined are too long or numerous to build a linear ramp system within the confined area. This could be used as a way to assess a student's understanding of the relationships between slope and speed and slope and direction.

Materials:

- Masking tape
- Tracks
- Spheres
- Unit blocks

Things that children can vary or change:

- The arrangement of track within the assigned "real estate"

Design constraints or things for the teacher to hold constant or the same:

- Taped-off areas of "real estate" small enough to require the design to include corners and drops
- A teacher-assigned number of tracks and sphere to use in constructing a ramp

Relationships children have the possibility of making:

- The constraint of space demands greater control of the marble's action
- Marbles that move slowly are easier to control than marbles that move quickly

Example of a teacher's introduction:

> *We just read about how architects are hired to build for other people, but have to listen closely to build what the people want. They can be creative, but they don't get to do whatever they want. Do you think that might be hard? Would some of you like to see what that might feel like?*

Example of questions and comments to inspire reasoning:

> *Which piece will start the marble?*
>
> *Which piece will come next?*
>
> *Where will you start your marble?*
>
> *Can you explain where you think the marble will go before you try your ramp out?*
>
> *How could you fill in any other parts of this area with ramp pieces that work?*
>
> *If you can't spread the ramp out any farther, is there a way to add pieces above?*
>
> *It seems to be going faster here, and here is where it always comes off. I wonder how that could be fixed?*

BUILDING VERTICAL RAMPS WITHIN A SMALL CONFINED AREA
(EXPERIENCED BUILDERS IN KINDERGARTEN AND UP)

By taping a narrow rectangle on the floor only slightly longer than a ramp section, builders can be challenged to conceptualize a vertical ramp system (see Photo 6.5). Children often believe the faster the marble goes, the better. However, in building vertical ramps, they may find that slowing the speed of the marble is the best way to build a successful system.

Photo 6.5. A Narrow Space Inspires a Design that Uses a Series of Vertical Drops to Get a Marble to Travel a Long Distance

Materials:

- Masking tape
- Unit blocks
- Standard size marbles
- Two same-sized lengths of track nearly as long as the taped-off rectangle

Things that children can vary or change:

- The steepness of the incline
- The design of the support structures

Design constraints or things for the teacher to hold constant or the same:

- Taped-off rectangles for work areas only slightly longer than the ramp sections to be used and no more than 1 foot wide

Relationships children have the possibility of making:

- Between the supports and how they serve both the starting end of one ramp and the receiving end of another
- Between the slope of the incline and control of the marble
- Between the speed and the force of the ricochet onto the next ramp section

Example of a teacher's introduction:

> *I once had a student figure out how to use both pieces in this small space. How do you suppose this could work?*

Questions to inspire reasoning:

> *If you think about getting the marble to change directions, how can you arrange the ramps?*

> *Can you make just one ramp work?*

> *If you leave that ramp alone, can you build a ramp above it and connect the two so they both work?*

> *Is there a way to add another level?*

> *How many sections high do you suppose you could build your system?*

BUILDING RAMPS WITH A FULCRUM AND BALANCE
(EXPERIENCED BUILDERS—TOWARD END OF 1ST GRADE AND UP)

By using a router to cut three grooves on the underside of several ramp sections and putting out triangle unit blocks to act as fulcrums, children are given a rich opportunity to reason about balance and distribution of weight (see Photo 6.6). Cutting three grooves underneath (one in the middle and two about an inch or 2 on either side) allows some choice and flexibility with balance. A groove in the exact middle allows the track to balance evenly. The grooves on either side allow the weight of the track to cause an incline, but as the marble travels up the incline and over the fulcrum, the added weight of the marble can cause the track to tip and create an incline in the opposite direction. This is fascinating to children and adds another level of design challenge.

Materials:

- Ramp sections with and without grooves routed on the bottom
- Triangular unit blocks for fulcrums
- Unit blocks
- Marbles

Things that children can vary or change:

- By this time, children often understand enough about the materials to decide what variables to control and what to keep constant. Children know how to integrate the challenge of moving tracks on fulcrums with their knowledge about how linear ramps, ramps with corners, and even vertical ramps work.

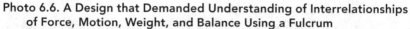

Photo 6.6. A Design that Demanded Understanding of Interrelationships of Force, Motion, Weight, and Balance Using a Fulcrum

Design constraints or things for the teacher to hold constant or the same:

- It may be best to start with a standard-size marble at the beginning. Later, marbles of different weights can be added.

Relationships children have the possibility of making:

- When a balance has one longer side, there is more weight on that side
- When there is the same amount of track at each end of the fulcrum, it balances
- Between the groove chosen to place upon the fulcrum and the distribution of the weight of the track
- Between the weight of the marble and the action of the balance
- Between the placement of the marble on the balancing ramp and the action of the balance (nearer to fulcrum, less action)
- Between the speed of the traveling marble and the action of the balance
- Between the height of the fulcrum and the track's degree of movement

Example of a teacher's introduction:

> *You are getting pretty good at building interesting ramp systems! I'm wondering how you might build a system with a moving track.*

[Demonstrate how to place a track on a fulcrum. Let them explore how this works with you.] *I'm going to leave these here with the rest of the tracks to see what you can do with them.*

Examples of questions and comments to inspire reasoning:

What do you need to think about when you are building this kind of ramp?

Where will the marble land on the track that is balancing?

What do you want the marble to do on the balance track?

Is there a special place you will need to put the balancing track on the fulcrum?

How will your ramp on the fulcrum move when the marble lands on the next ramp?

Where will the marble go after that?

Does it matter where you start your marble?

(After noticing a child has placed blocks restricting any movement of the balance) *When your ramp on the fulcrum cannot move, is it a balancing ramp, or is it a regular ramp with a triangle for a support? Is there something you can do to turn it into a balancing ramp?*

Can you get another working balancing track into your design?

MATHEMATICS WITHIN RAMPS AND PATHWAYS

The preceding examples of R&P challenges clearly exemplify the vision of the NGSS. Less obvious is the development of mathematics in R&P activities. Traditionally, kindergarten and the primary grades have focused on number. The Common Core State Standards (CCSS) recommend that children focus not only on number, but also on describing shapes and space, concepts heavily embedded in the work of R&P:

Students describe their physical world using geometric ideas (e.g., shape, orientation, spatial relations) and vocabulary. They identify, name, and describe basic two-dimensional shapes, such as squares, triangles, circles, rectangles, and hexagons, presented in a variety of ways (e.g., with different sizes and orientations), as well as three-dimensional shapes such as cubes, cones, cylinders, and spheres. They use basic shapes and spatial reasoning to model objects in their environment and to construct more complex shapes. (National Governors Association Center for Best Practices & Council of Chief State School Officers, 2010b, p. 9)

The CCSS go on to explain kindergartners should be able to describe and compare measureable attributes such as length or weight, and classify objects into categories (National Governors Association Center for Best Practices & Council of Chief State School Officers, 2010b). First-graders are further challenged to measure lengths indirectly and by iterating length units, reason with shapes and their attributes, and represent and interpret data (National Governors Association Center for Best Practices & Council of Chief State School Officers, 2010b). Second-graders are to examine sides and angles to describe and analyze shapes, decomposing and combining shapes to make other shapes. "Through building and analyzing two-and three-dimensional shapes, students develop a foundation for understanding area, volume, congruence, similarity, and symmetry" (National Governors Association Center for Best Practices & Council of Chief State School Officers, 2010b, p. 17). Reading through the previous R&P challenges, one can easily see how these mathematical standards can be presented to children within a context that makes sense to them. Although schools will not immediately see the value of challenging students in spatial thinking through R&P in 1st- or 2nd-grade standardized assessment scores, schools that encourage R&P will benefit in the long run. Longitudinal research suggests that the spatial reasoning developed through block building challenges like R&P in early childhood will predict high mathematics achievement at the 7th grade and high school levels (Casey, Andrews, Schindler, Kersh, & Samper, 2008; Casey, Nuttal, & Pezaris, 1997; Kersh, Casey, & Young, 2008; Wolfgang, Stannard, & Jones, 2001). STEM development starts early.

THE SYNERGY OF STEM AND LITERACY: A PERSONAL STORY

Kindergarten and primary grade teachers are finding it increasingly difficult to allocate instructional time to STEM activities such as R&P because of the pressures to perform well in literacy. My own personal struggle over this issue led me to redesign my classroom arrangement and use of time within the morning literacy block. In the process, I discovered the synergy of STEM and literacy. Adding STEM centers to the classroom did not distract from literacy learning, but instead enhanced it in ways I never imagined (Van Meeteren & Escalada, 2010).

In most kindergarten and primary grade classrooms, the day begins with whole-class literacy instruction and moves into small-group literacy instruction. Teachers often struggle with how to keep all children learning during this small-group instructional time. I met this challenge by offering three categories of activities to children during this block of time: teacher-directed small-group reading instruction, literacy investigations, and STEM investigations. Each category fulfilled different instructional and physical needs of young children. Offerings within each category had to stand up to the criteria: "What is in this activity for children to figure out, and is it worthy and respectful of their time?"

Teacher-directed small-group reading instruction enabled me to carefully focus on individual reading growth and progress. It required children to be intensely focused on problem solving in literacy and was located in a corner of the classroom. The children sat at a table with their backs to the action of the rest of the classroom to shield them from distractions. Sitting on the other side, I was able to survey the action of the whole classroom as I taught.

Nearby, the classroom library was arranged and stocked to inspire investigations into using the tools of reading, writing, viewing, speaking, and listening. Literacy investigations allowed children the space to develop positive literacy habits and skills. Children sat on beanbags or comfortable chairs in the midst of diverse genres of books and read to themselves or one another. They reread poems and songs they had previously enjoyed in whole-class literacy instruction; retold stories using puppets, figures, or flannel boards; or engaged in word work. Writing materials were nearby to allow them to record ideas and questions or compose skits, plays, or their own stories.

Across the room, well-equipped STEM investigations buzzed with activity and answered young children's need for movement and opportunities to be curious. Children engaged in the practices of science and engineering as they investigated questions in life science, earth and space science, and physical science (the context for R&P investigations). Throughout the STEM investigations area, tools for investigating were accessible and readily available for children (see Figure 6.1). Writing materials were close at hand to allow children to document their thinking, make lists of needed materials,

Figure 6.1. Children's Movement During Small-Group Literacy Instruction

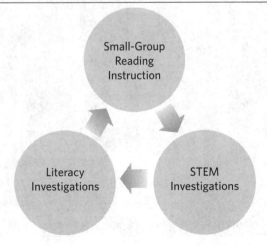

or create signs or messages to inform others what they were learning. Books children found in the classroom library that were pertinent to a specific investigation were placed close by for quick reference. It was an environment that provided purposes for children to *use* the tools of literacy and, in the process, created a desire within them to *learn* the tools of literacy.

Every week, I taught small-group reading instruction to specifically address literacy skills such as decoding, comprehension, and recognizing and using punctuation during guided reading. The groups rarely consisted of the same children. The children were divided daily into three sections. One section began in small-group reading instruction, one group in STEM investigations, and one group in literacy investigations. As I finished working with a small reading group, I asked each member what he or she wanted to figure out in the STEM investigations. After articulating a plan, each child went to begin his or her STEM investigation. I documented each child's intentions to follow his or her development as an independent investigator (see Photo 6.7).

Once the last child left the reading group to work on a STEM investigation, I walked through the classroom and observed the children who

Photo 6.7. Children Completing Work in Small-Group Reading and Preparing to Move to STEM Investigations

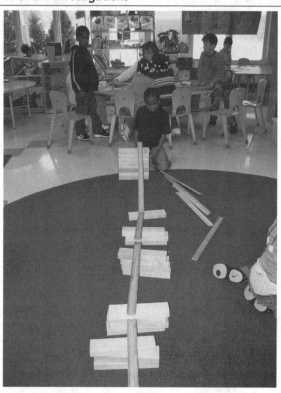

had been working in STEM investigations while I'd been teaching. After observing them at work, I had brief conversations with them to determine their conceptual understanding of science and engineering concepts as well as their development in scientific and engineering practices. I jotted notes about their development on Post-its, mailing labels, or in a notebook, and photographed children's progress with a digital camera. I used this documentation to track each child's progress in science and engineering practices as well as his or her understanding of disciplinary core ideas. The interactions gave me ideas on what we could discuss as a whole group. I reminded each child that when he or she reached a stopping point in the STEM investigation to clean up the space and move into literacy investigations in the classroom library. Some children began to clean up immediately, and others continued to ponder a problem a bit longer before cleaning up and moving on. Allowing children to wind up their investigations at their own pace enabled them to bring their work to completion, or to a satisfying stopping point. Forcing children who were on the cusp of figuring out a challenge they had been working on for half an hour to abruptly stop and move to a different area of the classroom would have caused unnecessary frustration. Giving children the responsibility of managing their time also helped them learn how to self-regulate their behavior.

After checking on each child in STEM investigations, I moved to the literacy investigations and invited children to join me for small-group reading instruction. Excited to share what they'd been figuring out in the classroom library, they were happy and eager to come to small-group instruction. The room was a productive hum of active learning.

R&P: A Pathway to Literacy

Many states are beginning to use the Common Core State Standards for English Language Arts & Literacy (National Governors Association Center for Best Practices & Council of Chief State School Officers, 2010a). These standards state that students need to have many opportunities to engage in conversations as part of a whole class, in small groups, and with partners. "Being productive members of these conversations requires that students contribute accurate, relevant information, respond to and develop what others have said; make comparisons and contrasts; and analyze and synthesize a multitude of ideas in various domains" (National Governors Association Center for Best Practices & Council of Chief State School Officers, 2010a), p. 22). R&P investigations provide a landscape where these conversations can occur. Documenting details of these important conversations inspires children to take on the challenge of developing print concepts, phonological awareness, and phonics and word recognition, all foundational skills within the Common Core (National Governors Association Center for Best Practices & Council of Chief State School Officers, 2010a). R&P investigations create an eagerness in children to write to share findings, demonstrating an understanding of what they are studying. They collaborate to create pieces of writing that convey their experiences and events, all goals within the Common Core writing standards (National Governors Association Center for Best Practices & Council of Chief State School Officers, 2010a).

Ramps and Pathways and Writers' Workshop

At the end of the morning, I typically set aside a 45- to 50-minute block for a writers' workshop. I began this block with a mini-lesson, followed by a period of quiet, individual writing, and concluded with a period of self-selected partner writing where children could use one another for help in spelling, topic choices, or word choice. We ended with a short author session where children, as authors, could share a personal draft or completed piece of writing. R&P investigations provided a context where children felt compelled to *use* the tool of written language to communicate what they were figuring out, which led to a desire to *learn* the tool of written language. Their desire to discuss and document their investigations launched meaningful writing mini-lessons that *interested* the children in writing; encouraged them to *explore* composition, spelling, and the mechanics of writing; and enabled them to *cooperate* with classmates to create and polish purposeful pieces of writing. For example, when children were adamant that they needed additional materials, the moment was ripe to launch a lesson on how to compose a list. Heavily invested in the purpose, the children would assist me in the process of composition by sharing their knowledge of phonemes and graphemes and spelling patterns to write the names of the materials on the list. They gave the list a title and directed me in the use of capital letters in the title. After composing the list, children often realized they needed help in acquiring items on the list. Thus, the next mini-lesson became an introduction on writing a letter to parents asking for help in collecting items on the list.

The digital photographs of action going on in the STEM investigations also are helpful in stimulating the desire to write. I often shared photos of what was going on in the R&P and expressed a desire to create a display or documentation board in the hallway for visitors to learn what we were figuring out. The mini-lesson evolved into writing captions for each picture. Children engaged in decisionmaking to sequence the pictures in the display to explain the process of their learning. In addition to assisting me with letter sounds and spelling patterns, children became adept at deciding where periods and capital letters were to be used in the captions.

Digital photographs were also useful in inspiring reluctant writers to write individual pieces. After creating a piece of lined writing paper with a blank space at the top, the paper can be fed through the printer to allow a digital picture of the writer at work in R&P. Referring to the picture at the top, the writer can use the space or lines at the bottom to write about his or her experience at the center. A series of pictures allows the writer to create an information piece that becomes a treasure to both the writer and the caregivers. It is a time capsule of a child's reasoning in his or her own words at a specific time of life.

When I was curious to find out where the children were in their reasoning, I often used the mini-lesson time to conduct interactive language experience stories based on children's experiences in the center. During brainstorming sessions, I recorded children's ideas and explanations of what they observed and understood, such as "Patterns We Noticed at the Ramp Center." I recorded misconceptions or misunderstandings as well as correct ideas so we could go back to previously written ideas and refine and revise them. This allowed children to understand that exploring science is a continuous learning process. Listening to children's misconceptions and explanations informed my instructional decisions and helped me create appropriate challenges. It allowed me to structure classroom discussions in ways that helped children confront their misconceptions about the different laws of physics. This gave a real reason to revise their understanding as well as their written records of thinking as they came to a better understanding of physics concepts. Revision became a necessity for the child instead of a requirement of the teacher.

As children became more sophisticated in their reasoning, I often used the mini-lesson to write a class piece on "What We Have Learned at the Ramp Center." The writing lesson focused on writing for a specific audience and was rich with possibilities for vocabulary expansion. As children offered ideas, they discussed and debated word choices and phrasing to allow the reader to fully understand the purpose of the center and what the children were accomplishing.

CONCLUSION

STEM should not be an exclusive plan of study that begins in upper elementary. Administrators and teachers should be respectful of STEM that already exists within young children's exploration of the world and support their investigations in STEM through activities such as R&P. Doing so will provide a firm foundation of interest and conceptual understanding for later learning in STEM. Administrators and early childhood teachers who are concerned about literacy achievement can feel secure in knowing that literacy development will flourish in a classroom environment that makes space for STEM and R&P. Ramps and Pathways investigations do not disrupt literacy development; rather, they breathe life and purpose into developing literacy as children speak, write, and read to explain their ideas about how the world works.

CHAPTER 7

Assessment

Jill Uhlenberg

This chapter will discuss issues in assessing children's learning and development in the domains of science, literacy, mathematics, and social development. The chapter begins with descriptions of different forms and purposes of assessment, followed by a brief look at what research tells us about assessment of young children. The third section addresses the Inquiry Teaching Model (ITM) and its relationship to assessment. Finally, this chapter will suggest multiple ways to complete assessments that focus on knowledge, skills, and dispositions, using both teacher-centered and student-centered processes and instruments.

For young children, the act of communicating with the teacher and with classmates will constitute multiple opportunities for assessment. Communication for preschool through 2nd-grade students involves developing language structures and building vocabulary—a major focus of learning in the early classroom, but we suggest that children need something about which to communicate. R&P provides an engaging and challenging activity that can serve as the context and content for gaining the communication skills that are so important to address in preschool and primary grades. The activities described in Chapter 4 are not only means of communicating; they are assessment documents in their own right. We will return to these communication documentation opportunities and discuss their relationship to assessment later in this chapter.

WHAT IS ASSESSMENT?

Assessment is actually a two-step process: documentation and evaluation. First, we need to gather evidence, and then we need to organize and interpret that evidence (McAfee, Leong, & Bodrova, 2004).

Teachers use many ways to document what children are learning, how they are progressing in building specific skills, how they are relating to one another, and more. For younger children who do not yet write well, observing and recording those observations are the basic means for teachers to document this growth. Even for primary age children, who are gaining literacy skills and are more able to use both oral and written expressive language (as described in Chapter 4), teacher observation remains an important piece of the assessment process, and the binding factor of all the components in the Inquiry Teaching Model.

During the second step in assessment—evaluation—teachers:

- review and reflect on the data,
- analyze what the data actually document,
- determine if they need additional documentation, and
- use the data to come to some conclusions.

Teachers need to use multiple sources of information about each child in this evaluation step (McAfee, Leong, & Bodrova, 2004; Puckett & Black, 2000). Some examples include anecdotal records, checklists, examples of student work, and other records of observations.

TYPES AND/OR PURPOSES OF ASSESSMENT

Assessments can be formal, using standardized tests or other valid and reliable instruments, or they can be informal and embedded within activities. These informal documents are also called authentic assessments. Each assessment provides a snapshot of a particular moment in a child's development. Just as we would never use a photograph of a child to try to describe fully what he or she is like, using a single assessment to evaluate a child's learning or development is inadequate and inappropriate. Fortunately, teachers have many opportunities to gather evidence about their students' learning throughout each day. The more evidence, the better we understand the child's current thinking and understanding.

Teachers need evidence for their decisionmaking regarding what to plan and teach, when to teach, and how to teach. Evidence also provides understanding about children's development over time, and whether they are progressing normally. That evidence is also needed for reporting to parents, colleagues, or administrators. Gathering evidence provides information for three purposes: diagnostic assessment, formative assessment, and summative assessment.

Diagnostic Assessment

The first purpose of assessment is diagnostic; that is, we gather evidence to find out what children already know or can do. This evidence informs our planning and teaching, especially when we differentiate instruction to address children's individual learning levels. Diagnostic assessment provides teachers with an understanding of the child's background knowledge so that teachers know where and when to push students to disequilibrium (as described in Chapter 2). For example, a 4-year-old created a very long pathway across a multipurpose room. He placed the first ramp segment against the wall to create an incline, and every segment after that he placed flat on the floor. When the marble slowed down and eventually stopped, he pushed it along the pathway and continued to add more segments. When the teacher asked him how he might be able to get the marble to continue rolling, he ignored her and continued to add ramp segments and push the marble. This told the teacher that he had not yet figured out the relationship between the height of the ramp and the movement of the marble. His actions also told the teacher that centration was still a primary factor in his problem-solving abilities; that is, he was unwilling to believe that his approach was not the correct one (Piaget, 1923/1959).

Formative Assessment

The second purpose of evidence gathering or documentation is for formative assessment, an opportunity for a teacher to gather information or evidence to inform his or her own teaching practice. Teachers gather multiple forms of evidence (which can include observations, questions that probe children's ideas, and so forth) during the processes of teaching and learning in order to make adjustments to what they have planned, to check for understanding, to document and monitor how children are progressing in their learning, and to provide documentation of this progress for reporting to parents or administrators. Formative assessments can be both formal and informal in nature.

Summative Assessment

Finally, evidence gathering is needed in the form of summative assessments. Once teachers complete a teaching unit or a project, or reach the end of the school year, they look at the collection of evidence to determine the students' long-term learning. Summative assessments are often tests or exams, looking at whether children have met a particular standard or benchmark, or attained a level of proficiency. However, summative assessment can also include such documentation as portfolios, end-of-year projects, or comparison with documents from early in the year.

Despite the descriptions of three different purposes or types of assessments, assessments and collected artifacts can be interchangeable between and among the types. How the teacher uses the information gathered will determine which type of assessment the data become.

Diagnostic assessment can be formative when a teacher uses that snapshot to consider what modifications or adaptations a particular child may need, and uses the assessment to guide instruction. The summative data at the end of a teaching unit are still formative assessment in that the teacher uses them to plan future teaching. Summative assessment indicates a final consideration for one teacher, but the information is actually formative for next year's teacher, or for the teacher in multiage classroom settings where children remain in the same classroom with the same teacher for more than one year.

To sum up this discussion, we could use the following criteria to distinguish the types and uses of assessment: (1) diagnostic—to identify existing ideas, skills, and learning difficulties; (2) formative—to inform instruction and provide feedback to children; and (3) summative—to measure and document student learning and performance. Regardless of the label, the main issue is how we *use* the evidence we have collected.

RESEARCH AND ASSESSMENT

NAEYC's (2009) position statement *Where We Stand on Curriculum, Assessment, and Program Evaluation* indicates the following criteria for the appropriate assessment of learning: "To best assess young children's strengths, progress, and needs, use assessment methods that are developmentally appropriate, culturally and linguistically responsive, tied to children's daily activities, supported by professional development, inclusive of families, and connected to specific, beneficial purposes" (p. 1). Although the NGSS do not address assessment directly, these standards advocate for assessment of learning based on performance: "Student performance expectations have to include a student's ability to apply a practice to content knowledge. Performance expectations thereby focus on understanding and application as opposed to memorization of facts devoid of context" (NRC, 2013). The NGSS also reflect a shift to conceptual understanding that is developed over months and years, rather than days and weeks. This shift is an integral component of the authors' approach toward STEM learning in the early years.

Jones (2011) charges educators to think about assessment systems as integral to teaching and learning rather than as separate and stand-alone instruments. She believes that assessment is too complex a task to leave to a single instrument because young children demonstrate individual variability of growth and development in the cognitive, physical, and social-emotional domains. In addition, the differences between and among children's physical, psychological, and cultural status, and their varied approaches to learning, all point to using multiple assessments. Such assessment systems should also be in alignment with appropriate learning standards, so that teachers know what to assess.

Boardman (2007) asserts that current approaches to assessment records and documentation are often a deficit model of assessment; that is, it is assessment about what learners *cannot* do, rather than what they *can* do. Instead, Boardman recommends using three lenses in gathering evidence about both what children can and cannot do, and in the teacher's reflection and evaluation of that evidence:

- *Intrapersonal lens:* looking at the child as an individual
- *Interpersonal lens:* looking at the child within the group
- *Contextual lens:* looking at the child in the classroom environment

Such an approach requires the use of multiple forms of documentation in order to view the child and his or her learning from these three different perspectives. With this systems approach, teachers can build a comprehensive and complex picture of children's learning and development over time in their classrooms.

Classrooms in formal settings, such as public or private schools, licensed preschools, or Head Start programs, have assessment systems in place that document this variability among young children. Meaningful evaluation of the evidence about children's learning will be completed using required assessment forms and teachers' knowledge of the children in their classrooms.

ASSESSMENT AND THE INQUIRY TEACHING MODEL

In earlier chapters, we discussed the teacher's role in observing children's behaviors and conversations. In early childhood settings, the teacher's observation is the primary means of gathering information about children's learning. If observation is equated with assessment, even loosely, then the ITM is immersed in assessment. At every step in the interactive processes of Engaging Learners, Providing Opportunities, and Making Informed Decisions, assessment plays a key role. The different components and assessment are intertwined so that it is difficult to look at any one segment of the model without considering how it is connected to assessment.

Engagement

Teachers engage learners by using diagnostic assessment, identifying the interests of a particular child or group of children, what they already know about that topic, the skills they have already developed, and the kinds of experiences they have had. Typically, not all children will be at the same place on the learning continuum, which challenges the teacher in evaluating the evidence and then deciding how to proceed. For example, in a kindergarten classroom, some children will arrive in the fall with no prior out-of-home experiences at all, while others will have had up to 5 years of child care and preschool experiences. The most successful materials for such a wide span of skill and knowledge are open-ended; that is, activities such as R&P allow children to construct both concepts and skills from where they are without having to stop and review. The materials are also engaging and allow for teachers to provoke children's natural curiosity.

Informed Decisions

Teachers make informed decisions based on the evidence they gather in the diagnostic assessments. Once we understand what children know and can do, we develop ways to promote deeper thinking about R&P and the ways objects work in the physical world. Additionally, R&P provides opportunities to think more deeply in other subject or academic areas, including literacy, mathematics, social studies, and social-emotional development. Such interventions include asking productive questions (see Chapter 2) that stimulate students' problem-solving skills and communication skills, and that provide the teacher an opportunity to check for students' understanding. Those interventions will provide additional formative assessment information as teachers ask students to document what they are learning in a variety of ways.

These informed decisions regarding planning cover the spectrum of the curriculum. Mathematical learning, for example, may focus on any of the five areas within the Common Core State Standards for Mathematics (2010). Figure 7.1 illustrates how the R&P activities in kindergarten address mathematical learning.

Examples of literacy-based authentic assessments are discussed in Chapter 4, "Ramps and Pathways Promote Communication Development." Teacher-made reporting forms can be designed to include specific literacy goals and objectives. In addition, checklists, anecdotal records, photographs, recorded video segments, and conversations might be valuable resources for assessing literacy development.

Opportunities to Learn

Once teachers decide how to proceed in challenging their students' thinking about R&P, they will provide additional challenges, designed for the developmental level of the child or group, that will encourage success while triggering further exploration. An example of the model and how assessment works throughout the different components occurred in one combined 1st-/2nd-grade classroom. According to the 1st-/2nd-grade teacher, she observed that the students seemed to be engaging more in other areas of the classroom and less with R&P. When a child did work in the ramps center, he or she often

Figure 7.1. Kindergarten Mathematics Assessment Possibilities

R&P Mathematics Activity	Concepts	Mathematics CCSS Met/ Addressed
Collect and count objects from classroom to explore which roll down a ramp and which do not roll; record on a T chart	Counting Comparison Classifying	Counting and cardinality Measurement and data Number and operations in base 10
Count objects from classroom by classification (color, type, wheeled, and so on) categories; tally categories and compare on chart	Counting Classifying Comparing	Counting and cardinality Number and operations in base 10 Operations and algebraic thinking Measurement and data
Compare different weight marbles on a balance; compare distance marbles roll	Comparison Classifying	Measurement and data
Compare different lengths of ramp pieces; compose longer lengths from shorter lengths of ramp pieces	Counting Comparison Composing shapes	Counting and cardinality Number and operations in base 10 Measurement and data Geometry
Compare distances different marbles roll on the same ramp	Comparison Measurement	Measurement and data
Compare distance the same marble rolls on different ramps; photograph ramps and identify triangles constructed; compare triangles	Comparison Measurement Identifying shapes Comparing shapes	Measurement and data Geometry
Construct ramps that include angles or corners	Analyzing two-/three-dimensional shapes	Geometry
Construct ramps with target to catch marble; compare marbles and differences in location of target	Comparison Measurement	Measurement and data Geometry

stayed only briefly, constructing structures that were commonly seen in other children's pathway constructions, and without much complexity or innovation. This assessment led this teacher to consider how she might stimulate new interest while also pushing the students to try new ways of using the R&P materials. She taped off areas on the classroom floor and challenged children at center time to construct a ramp pathway within that space. Because the taped-off areas were only 3–4 feet long and wide, the students were forced to think about how they could build taller ramps rather than the longer versions they had been regularly constructing across the classroom.

During this new construction phase, the teacher frequently visited the students as they worked, asking questions to probe their planning and to evoke ways to communicate to other children what they were accomplishing. This step in the teacher's facilitation of R&P investigations integrated mathematics (spatial relationships), engineering (designing new structures), literacy skills (communicating results or problems), and social development. The challenge reignited the students' interest in R&P and provided additional assessment data through observations and anecdotal records, as well as through students' products of documentation.

The Inquiry Teaching Model, with its three interactive components, is clearly also a model for ongoing assessment. Opportunities for evidence collection are inherent in each section, giving the classroom teacher a variety of products and evidence with which to continue planning and evaluating students' learning.

WHAT TO ASSESS

Teachers must be wary of how many skills, sets of knowledge, or dispositions they will want to assess. First priority should fall to school or program standards and requirements—typically content knowledge. For science areas, scientific and engineering practices such as observing, communicating, and classifying are also vital learning for young children, although teachers often expect that, developmentally, students are typically able to demonstrate a limited number of science processes during the preschool-to-2nd-grade age range.

Science Knowledge and Science Practices

As noted in Chapter 3, younger children are not able to demonstrate the same science practices or levels of understanding as older students. They can, however, learn to clearly demonstrate their understanding. The most appropriate science practices to assess, and ones we have been successful with, depending on preschoolers', kindergartners', and primary age children's experiences, are observing, communicating, measuring, and classifying. With teacher guidance and facilitation of controlling variables, they can begin to investigate their ideas and explorations of how the materials work. Developing these science practices through a practical understanding of the science behind R&P will be a foundation for later learning, and more thorough development of science processes and content.

The *Head Start Child Development and Early Learning Framework* (2010) addresses the science knowledge and practices important for children 3 to 5 years old. The focus is on emerging abilities and curiosity, asking questions, and refining understanding through exploration of materials. The framework focuses on two domain elements for preschool-age children: (1) scientific skills and method, and (2) conceptual knowledge of the natural and physical world (see Figure 7.2). Embedded within these two elements are ideas for assessing learning that are appropriate for the age and developmental levels of preschoolers.

Figure 7.2. Head Start Child Development and Early Learning Framework Elements

---

Scientific Skills & Method: The skills to observe and collect information and use it to ask questions, predict, explain, and draw conclusions.

- Uses senses and tools, including technology, to gather information, investigate materials, and observe processes and relationships.

- Observes and discusses common properties, differences, and comparisons among objects.

- Participates in simple investigations to form hypotheses, gather observations, draw conclusions, and form generalizations.

- Collects, describes, and records information through discussions, drawings, maps, and charts.

- Describes and discusses predictions, explanations, and generalizations based on past experience.

Conceptual Knowledge of the Natural & Physical World: The acquisition of concepts and facts related to the natural and physical world and the understanding of naturally occurring relationships.

- Observes, describes, and discusses living things and natural processes.

- Observes, describes, and discusses properties of materials and transformation of substances.

Source: Head Start Child Development and Early Learning Framework, 2010.

More challenging to assess, although vitally important among the 21st-century skills (www.skills21.org), are children's problem-solving abilities. These are abilities that support more flexible responses to change and that stimulate innovation. Even more difficult to assess are children's dispositions for learning and enjoying science, and the development of *executive function*, or the ability to control one's behavior and thinking through a strong working memory, taking others' perspectives, and attending to an activity or event.

Problem Solving

Several components make up the practice of problem solving, which leads again to the need for systems of assessment, rather than a single tool or instrument. Keen (2010) suggests that problem solving includes perception, cognition, and motor development, but argues that even language and attachment are related. With young children, who may have difficulty explaining why something has happened, we often must rely on observations of children's behaviors to infer their intent in terms of planning and carrying out intentional actions. It is important for the teacher to ask children what problem they are working on in order to observe the development of an appropriate solution. Again, the use of productive questions supports teachers' ability to do this (see Chapter 3). If the teacher does not know the child's agenda, he or she may make incorrect assumptions about how effectively the children did (or did not) solve the problem.

Preschool- and kindergarten-age children often fail to anticipate a problem in R&P until it happens. Or they fail to perceive that a problem even exists in some cases. This means that finding the problem is the first step to problem solving, and teachers play a role in facilitating this step for young children. A child may experience a marble leaving the pathway consistently at the same spot without realizing the regularity. A teacher may be able to focus the child's attention to that spot through questioning, so that the child can be the problem solver.

Often, children will adjust one connection between ramp pieces without understanding that moving one end may also move the opposite end. This is an indication that the child is focusing only on one aspect of the ramp at a time, and does not view it as a system. Knowing this, the teacher can use questions and comments to draw the child's attention to both ends of the ramp. Sometimes children notice that a problem exists, but do nothing to change the outcome. Teacher support through comments and questions can provide incentive for the child to make adjustments without becoming frustrated in the process. Eventually, children will learn to systematically try different solutions until they find one that works to solve the problem (Diamond, 2005). These activities are clearly addressed in the NGSS, with connections to engineering in the crosscutting concept of cause and effect (see Figure 7.3). Each NGSS provides a Clarification Statement with examples of how students can understand and apply the science concept in meaningful ways.

Future-oriented thinking, or planning ahead to consider unknowns, is very difficult for young children and takes time to develop. Understanding this series of steps in the development of children's problem-solving ability will help the teacher make careful observations that will lead to further interactions and manipulating materials in productive ways to accomplish children's goals in building R&P.

Dispositions

Dispositions to learn are typically defined as persistence, curiosity, willingness to collaborate, and (in classrooms where R&P are involved) a comfort level with science. In addition, three others—inhibitory control, working memory, and attention—are typically described as making up *executive function*. Executive function (EF) has been found to be extremely important in children's development. Several recent research reports suggest that preschoolers and kindergartners with stronger EF achieve higher levels of school success generally than children with lower EF (Brock, Rimm-Kaufman, Nathanson, & Grimm, 2009; Lan, Legare, Ponitz, Li, & Morrison, 2011; McClelland, Cameron, Wanless, & Murray, 2007).

Figure 7.3. Example *Next Generation Science Standards* with Clarification Statements

Motion and Stability: Forces and Interactions
Students who demonstrate understanding can do the following:

K-PS2-1. Plan and conduct an investigation to compare the effects of different strengths or different directions of pushes and pulls on the motion of an object. [Clarification Statement: Examples of pushes or pulls could include a string attached to an object being pulled, a person pushing an object, a person stopping a rolling ball, and two objects colliding and pushing on each other.] [*Assessment Boundary: Assessment is limited to different relative strengths or different directions, but not both at the same time. Assessment does not include non-contact pushes or pulls such as those produced by magnets.*]

K-PS2-2. Analyze data to determine if a design solution works as intended to change the speed or direction of an object with a push or a pull. [Clarification Statement: Examples of problems requiring a solution could include having a marble or other object move a certain distance, follow a particular path, and knock down other objects. Examples of solutions could include tools such as a ramp to increase the speed of the object and a structure that would cause an object such as a marble or ball to turn.] [*Assessment Boundary: Assessment does not include friction as a mechanism for change in speed.*]

Again, teacher observation and conversations with students are the most productive ways to assess children's dispositions. Formal instruments have been developed to assess these dispositions specifically; however, most classroom teachers do not have the skill or time to complete these assessment instruments. A checklist we developed gives teachers an example of how assessing children's R&P skill and disposition growth might be accomplished (see Appendix 7.1).

One of the main concerns about assessing dispositions, Bone (2001) argues, is that dispositions are very open to interpretation. Bone also cautions that teachers must remain aware that demonstrating dispositions may also be culturally variable; that is, cultures that diminish the individual in favor of the group's welfare may teach children to refrain from demonstrating socially or emotionally what they are feeling.

Despite these cautions, multiple forces in the field of teacher preparation and STEM education continue to look to dispositions as an important component to develop, both in teachers and in learners (Committee on Highly Successful Schools, 2011; Council of Chief State School Officers, 2011). And if they are important to develop, then the dispositions are also important to assess.

HOW TO ASSESS

Documenting learning may be done by the teacher or by the learners. Each has specific value and will likely yield different information.

Teacher-Centered Assessments

The teacher uses formal instruments, such as the Iowa Tests of Basic Skills (ITBS), as well as informal assessments, including anecdotal records and checklists. Deciding which to use will depend on several decision points for the teacher. First, if a specific assessment is required, that is the means teachers will use. However, if there is flexibility in deciding, the teacher will want to ask him-/herself the following questions before making the decision:

- What specific action or skill am I assessing?
- How specific do I need to be given the time available?
- Am I assessing one child or the group?
- Am I assessing for current skill or am I assessing for growth in a skill?
- Am I experienced enough to complete this data collection? (McAfee, Leong, & Bodrova, 2004)

Completing assessments one-on-one with children will yield the most information about individuals. However, other assessments will be more efficient in terms of teachers' time while still yielding adequate information. In addition, the purpose of the assessment (diagnostic, formative, or summative) will be integral to the decision of which format to use. In all cases, the assessment chosen must be one that allows the teacher to learn whether children are meeting the planned objectives of the activities.

Teacher-made assessments include many ways of documenting learning and gathering evidence, and typically focus on descriptions, counting or tallying, and rating or ranking (McAfee, Leong, & Bodrova, 2004). Narrative records take substantial time to write, but anecdotal records, sketches, diagrams, and minimalistic reminders on sticky notes yield high-quality information if teachers take care to record objectively what they observe. Evaluation of what is observed comes later, after all the evidence is gathered. The use of digital photography and video can greatly enhance and expedite this process. With simple still and video cameras available at reasonable cost, teachers can take photographs and videos of children working. Teachers may add notes or children's dictations to the printed photo to explain their learning, list standards being met, or document the need for additional practice or materials.

Means of counting or tallying may include teacher checklists, charts, or tables that state whether a child has completed a task or has demonstrated a skill. Rating scales that depict a child's level of competency (*rarely, often, always*) as well as checklists can be constructed quickly on computer spreadsheets. In addition, teachers may modify the previous form (see Appendix 7.1) by putting children's names in the columns across the top of the page and simply coding a *not yet* (N), *sometimes* (S), or *consistently* (C) in the column next to each skill or behavior being assessed. This allows for collecting information on the whole class.

Learning records provide teachers a means of recording their observations. In their inquiry-based Young Scientist Series, including *Building Structures with Young Children*, Chalufour and Worth (2004) offer examples of ways to document children's science learning. Van Meeteren (2014) has adapted those forms to address assessment within R&P. The assessments include science and engineering processes and engineering habits of mind outcomes that emerge from children's R&P activities, thus expanding the science assessment to include engineering. The outcome charts (see Appendixes 7.2 and 7.3) support teachers' understanding of the recording forms and help them anticipate the need for extended learning or development of social skills related to working with others in the classroom.

Brainstorming charts, also called mind maps, developed by the teacher alone or with children, will provide a good foundation for discerning learning goals on which to focus during any particular course of study. K-W-L charts, completed together with students will document what the children already *know* (K), what they *want* to know (W), and revisited later, what they have *learned* (L).

Rubrics are another means of documenting learning. Well-developed rubrics allow teachers to clearly delineate what parameters the children must meet to be considered proficient.

An important strategy for R&P teachers to dig more deeply into children's learning, and to add to the descriptive data for individual children, is to use productive questions. Descriptions and examples of the different kinds of questions teachers can ask are discussed in Chapter 3. Recording such questions and the children's responses can provide yet another source of data about children's knowledge, skills, and dispositions.

Helpful tools for assessment also include charts of learning outcomes or expectations that are cross-referenced with science or engineering concepts. For the R&P project, we designed an outcomes chart that linked children's behaviors with science concepts that we observed in the children's designing and construction of pathways (see Appendix 7.4). Our expectations were for a practical understanding of Newton's Laws as well as the principles of designing and investigating different constructions, rather than a formal knowledge of science and engineering concepts.

We also designed an outcomes chart that linked children's behaviors to engineering habits of mind (see Appendix 7.5). Such charts provide valuable resources for teachers' ability to define and observe for specific behaviors that relate to STEM learning.

Child-Centered Assessments

Studying children's products provides a separate means of gathering information about what children have learned. In Chapter 4, we offer suggestions on how children can document their work on ramps. These products are clear examples of the *embedded* evidence of learning that are pieces of the assessment puzzle. Each document can provide assessment data in multiple academic and developmental areas, such as emerging literacy skills, science content, social skills of collaboration or cooperation, mathematical understanding of spatial relationships and measurement, and more. These embedded assessments provide readily accessible information about children's learning without having to develop a separate assessment tool or instrument.

Drawings are most common for preschoolers and young kindergartners, and are an early form of writing to communicate information. Teachers may add dictation text when the child discusses his or her representation of the ramp. (Read more about children's communication during R&P in Chapters 4 and 6.)

Even before formal writing abilities emerge, children can draw and write in science journals, and share what they know or want to know about ramps and pathways. In addition, children can use their drawings as demonstration materials in explaining their work to other children, as well as communicating that information verbally.

Other student products include photographs, clay models, or demonstrations, which provide alternate ways for children to communicate what they have learned about R&P. Products in which students have choices about delivery also provide opportunities for students to consider and reflect upon their own work. Teachers often forget about students completing self-assessments, especially young children, or they assume these children are not yet able to complete self-assessments. However, children can develop reflectivity about their work, with support and role models within the classroom, so that they can learn to assess their own progress and set goals for ongoing work with ramps and pathways.

CONCLUSION

In this chapter, we have described only a few of the many opportunities for teachers to gather data about what children can learn using R&P materials in a preschool–2nd-grade classroom setting. We have demonstrated the inseparable relationship between assessment and the ITM, and offered some examples of embedded and authentic assessments of children's learning that we have used in our work with R&P.

APPENDIX 7.1. RAMPS & PATHWAYS CHECKLIST

Name: _____   Date: _____

Complete this checklist **for each child in your classroom** three times during the school year (roughly every 12 weeks). Circle the letter that corresponds to the child's level of performance.

N = Not Yet
S = Sometimes
C = Consistently

Ramps & Pathways Checklist	1st Trimester	2nd Trimester	3rd Trimester
1. Engages with R&P activities that lead to the movement of an object—may or may not include direct contact with the materials.	N S C	N S C	N S C
2. Communicates verbally or nonverbally an awareness of an object's movement on a ramp structure.	N S C	N S C	N S C
3. Tries an idea (stated or unstated) about the movement of an object on ramps.	N S C	N S C	N S C
4. When an object does not move as expected, changes something and tries again.	N S C	N S C	N S C
5. Makes changes in ramp *structure* to address problems that prevent objects from moving as desired (not necessarily successful).	N S C	N S C	N S C
6. Describes how an object moves on ramp structure through telling, demonstrating, or drawing.	N S C	N S C	N S C
7. Shows or tells another person what to do to make an object move as desired.	N S C	N S C	N S C
8. When unsuccessful in making an object move as desired, persists in seeking a solution to the problem; that is, pursues purpose in the face of "failure."	N S C	N S C	N S C

(continued)

Appendix 7.1. *(continued)*

Ramps & Pathways Checklist	1st Trimester			2nd Trimester			3rd Trimester		
9. Devises or accepts a new challenge/ problem or adds a new level of complexity to existing structure to make an object move as desired.	N	S	C	N	S	C	N	S	C
10. Demonstrates positive attitudes connected to ramps and pathways.	N	S	C	N	S	C	N	S	C
11. Shows confidence in the ability to make an object move on ramp structures as desired.	N	S	C	N	S	C	N	S	C
12. Successfully manipulates ramps structure to make an object move as desired without striking or blowing the object.	N	S	C	N	S	C	N	S	C
13. Makes incremental changes to one variable in order to create a desired change in the movement of the object.	N	S	C	N	S	C	N	S	C
14. Anticipates potential difficulties in making an object move as desired and makes necessary changes prior to releasing object on ramps structure.	N	S	C	N	S	C	N	S	C

APPENDIX 7.2. OBSERVATIONAL RECORD: R&P CONSTRUCTIONS

Teacher: _____ Date: _____

Setting: _____

Check one: ☐ open exploration ☐ focused exploration

Design Challenge(s): ☐ incline ☐ hill ☐ jump ☐ drop
☐ loop ☐ corner ☐ switchback ☐ target ☐ fulcrum ☐ other

Children's Names	Seen and Heard

Adapted from *Building Structures with Young Children* by Ingrid Chalufour & Karen Worth. Copyright © 2004 by Ingrid Chalufour & Karen Worth. Reprinted with permission of Redleaf Press, St. Paul, MN; www.redleafpress.org.

APPENDIX 7.3. LEARNING RECORD: ENGINEERING BEHAVIORS

Child: _____ Birth Date: _____

Date Exploration Begun:_____ Completed:_____

Engineering Behaviors	Child Growth	Evidence
Poses own design problems	☐ Emerging ☐ Sometimes ☐ Consistently	
Locates and gathers materials; uses materials in a variety of ways	☐ Emerging ☐ Sometimes ☐ Consistently	
Notices, observes, and analyzes areas of failure	☐ Emerging ☐ Sometimes ☐ Consistently	
Views failures as an opportunity to problem-solve and perseveres	☐ Emerging ☐ Sometimes ☐ Consistently	
Tests in an iterative fashion to make sure sections or whole system works	☐ Emerging ☐ Sometimes ☐ Consistently	
Consults others	☐ Emerging ☐ Sometimes ☐ Consistently	
Offers and/or provides assistance to others in their design problems	☐ Emerging ☐ Sometimes ☐ Consistently	
Explains design and communicates through oral or written documentation	☐ Emerging ☐ Sometimes ☐ Consistently	

Adapted from *Building Structures with Young Children* by Ingrid Chalufour & Karen Worth. Copyright © 2004 by Ingrid Chalufour & Karen Worth. Reprinted with permission of Redleaf Press, St. Paul, MN; www.redleafpress.org.

APPENDIX 7.4. LEARNING RECORD:
SCIENCE CONTENT KNOWLEDGE

Child: _____ Birth Date: _____

Date Exploration Begun:_____ Completed:_____

Science Concepts	Child Growth	Evidence
Forces—A force is a "push" or "pull" acting on an object.		
A force requires two objects to interact.	☐ Emerging	
A child pushes a marble with his or her finger.	☐ Sometimes	
	☐ Consistently	
A marble dropped from some height.		
A marble rolling down a ramp.		
Notices properties of objects and how the properties affect movement.	☐ Emerging ☐ Sometimes ☐ Consistently	
Notices and describes different types of movement.	☐ Emerging ☐ Sometimes ☐ Consistently	
Working understanding of Newton's First Law: An object at rest remains at rest and an object in motion will continue to move steadily in a straight line unless acted upon by outside force.	☐ Emerging ☐ Sometimes ☐ Consistently	
An object has "inertia"—tendency to resist changes in its state of motion or nonmotion. The more "inertia" an object has, the more resistance.		
Working understanding of Newton's Second Law:	☐ Emerging ☐ Sometimes ☐ Consistently	
An unbalanced or net force acting on an object will result in the object to speed up, slow down, and/or change direction.		
Working understanding of Newton's Third Law:	☐ Emerging ☐ Sometimes ☐ Consistently	
For every action, there is an equal but opposite reaction.		

Adapted from *Building Structures with Young Children* by Ingrid Chalufour & Karen Worth. Copyright © 2004 by Ingrid Chalufour & Karen Worth. Reprinted with permission of Redleaf Press, St. Paul, MN; www.redleafpress.org.

APPENDIX 7.5. ENGINEERING HABITS OF MIND OUTCOMES

Term	NRC (2008) Definition of Engineering Habits of Mind	Engineering Habits of Mind Behaviors in Young Children
Systems Thinking	Equips students to recognize essential interconnections in the technological world Appreciates that systems may have unexpected effects that cannot be predicted from the behavior of individual subsystems	Adjusts both ends of a track After adjusting one component, coordinates positions of other components before testing
Creativity	Inherent (part of the very nature of something, and therefore permanently characteristic of it or necessarily involved in it)	Generates own design Flips, rotates, or repurposes materials Considers different ways of arranging supports, tracks, barriers Resists premature closure by continuing to add to complexity even after a successful test
Optimism	A world view in which possibilities and opportunities can be found in every challenge An understanding that every technology can be improved	Does not abandon structure after a failed test Uses failed tests as opportunities to find solutions Tries again after multiple failed tests
Collaboration	Leverages the perspectives, knowledge, and capabilities of team members to address a design challenge	Asks for help from a peer Considers suggestions of a peer Asks to test a peer's system Uses peer's system as a model Provides encouragement and/or advice to a peer
Communication	Essential to effective collaboration Essential to understanding the particular wants of a customer Essential to explain and justify the final design solution	Shares success of structure with peer Explains success of structure to a peer Asks for help and discusses problem with peer Offers advice to a peer Volunteers to build for another and asks what the peer wants in a design Writes or draws about system

	Draws attention to the impacts of engineering on people	
Attention to Ethical Considerations	Draws attention to the impact of engineering on the environment	Coordinates use of space with peers
	Considers possible unintended consequences of technology	Coordinates use of materials with peers
	Considers the potential disproportionate advantages and disadvantages of technology for certain groups or individuals	Takes responsibility for knock-downs
		Considers safety

Adapted from *Building Structures with Young Children* by Ingrid Chalufour & Karen Worth. Copyright © 2004 by Ingrid Chalufour & Karen Worth. Reprinted with permission of Redleaf Press, St. Paul, MN; www.redleafpress.org.

CHAPTER 8

Ramps and Pathways Professional Development

Creating Early STEM Communities of Practice

Shelly Counsell

The amount, scope, and quality of early childhood professional development (PD) have long been criticized as "inconsistent, fragmented, and often chaotic" (NRC, 2001). According to the National Child Care Information and Technical Assistance Center (2011), only 16 states require any preservice requirements for child-care center teachers (17 states have requirements for master teachers), while 48 states require ongoing annual training hours. Only 11 states mandate preservice requirements for small family child-care providers (15 states have requirements for large family child-care providers), while 39 states require ongoing annual training hours for small family child-care providers (37 states for large child-care providers). According to the U.S. Bureau of Labor Statistics (2014), the median hourly wages for child-care workers and preschool teachers (excluding special education) are $10.44 and $15.40 respectively, compared to a mean annual wage of $53,480 for kindergarten teachers (www.bls.gov/oes/home.htm).

Regardless of the impact that minimal standards, poor wages, and benefits have on the field, early childhood educators are held accountable for providing high-quality care and education for young children. The vast range of educational backgrounds and professional experiences among early childhood educators translates into a wide assortment of strengths and needs that complicate any effort to effectively provide adequate PD. In science alone, most early childhood and primary grade teachers place a low priority on science teaching (Skamp & Mueller, 2001). Raizen (1988) reported that the amount of time spent on science in grades kindergarten through grade 3 on a weekly basis averaged only 18 minutes. Almost 2 decades later, on average, only 6–13% of instructional time is allocated to science teaching in grades 1–4 (National Institute of Child Health and Human

Development, 2005). By 4th grade, only one-third of students (34%) perform at or above a proficient level in science according to *The Nation's Report Card: Science 2009* (National Center for Education Statistics, 2011). The previous chapters in this guide focused on explaining *how* to best instruct young children according to the Inquiry Teaching Model (ITM). In contrast, the purpose of this chapter is to examine Ramps and Pathways (R&P) from the perspective of the *adult* learner and to address how best to prepare education professionals as early STEM educators within STEM communities of practice. Teachers typically depend on PD workshops to provide the necessary skills and knowledge needed to increase their expertise and improve teaching practice. To satisfy the urgent need to provide PD in the area of early STEM, the Regents' Center for Early Developmental Education at the University of Northern Iowa has developed an R&P professional development program with two key components: (1) an introductory 3-hour R&P workshop for early childhood educators developed to provide a foundation in early STEM education and (2) the implementation of STEM learning communities of practice for ongoing STEM learning and PD.

The NRC (2007) identified teacher knowledge, teachers' opportunities to learn, and instructional systems as the three most critical components influencing children's science learning. The first goal of this chapter is to provide an overview of the R&P 3-hour introductory workshop, outlining the content, activities, and contact information. The second goal is to support educators' efforts to create STEM learning communities of practice with colleagues in the workplace in order to maintain and expand upon educators' ongoing STEM learning, understanding, and subsequent teaching practice using R&P activities with young children.

R&P INTRODUCTORY WORKSHOP

Research has demonstrated that the amount of time and the quality of science learning experiences provided to young children directly correspond with teachers' science content knowledge (Marx & Harris, 2006). Educators who have a strong grasp of science concepts and inquiry teaching practice spend more time and provide higher-quality science learning experiences for young children.

Because educators generally teach in the same manner in which they were taught as learners (Stoddart, Connell, Stofflett, & Peck, 1993), educators who have not experienced inquiry teaching and active experimentation as learners are less likely to use inquiry strategies as educators. If teaching practices are based on educators' prior experiences as learners, then transforming teaching practice in science for many early childhood educators will require providing new STEM learning experiences that embrace inquiry and engage educators in active exploration, investigation, and experimentation.

As an alternative to the typical stand-and-deliver, one-shot workshops presented by science experts who lecture while adult learners listen passively (NRC, 2007), R&P professional development envisions a long-term scope for change in early STEM teaching and learning that reaches far beyond the careers of individual participants in order to make change that encompasses *entire* learning communities. According to the U.S. Department of Education's (2010) literature review examining features of effective PD for early childhood educators, research has identified an initial set of six strategies that are also integral to the design and implementation of R&P professional development:

1. Specific objectives are articulated for PD. The R&P 3-hour introductory workshop was developed specifically with five key components: (1) rich science curriculum, (2) engagement in constructivist inquiry-based experiences, (3) experiences that include a wide range of engaging materials, (4) practical information about the teacher's role as facilitator, and (5) the expansion of a teacher's science content knowledge and understanding. Beyond the workshop, educators are encouraged to create and participate in STEM communities of practice to continue practicing, expanding, and supporting community members' efforts to implement R&P with young children.

2. Practice is an explicit focus of the PD, and attention is given to linking the focus on early educator knowledge and practice. R&P professional development recognizes that educators cannot be expected to design and implement STEM learning activities (explorations and investigations) that fully utilize inquiry teaching practice with young children if they have no firsthand experience engaging in these kinds of STEM activities as STEM learners. The R&P introductory workshop and STEM communities of practice afford educators the opportunity to experience scientific thinking as science learners, providing the insight and perspective they need to plan and implement meaningful STEM activities. "Only then can teachers (who are prepared to think scientifically, analyze phenomena, and engage in meaningful discourse with peers) successfully connect science-learning experiences in ways that reinvent science-teaching practice" (Counsell, 2011, p. 54).

3. There is collective participation of teachers from the same classrooms or schools in PD. State-level and district-level agencies and programs (for example, area education agencies, Child Care Resource and Referral Network participants, and Head Start), professional groups (such as NAEYC Chapter Affiliates), and public school systems often schedule workshop sessions for a cohort of early childhood educators. Whenever possible, two or more educators representing each school or program are encouraged to attend the introductory workshop together. However, budget restrictions may impede professionals from participating and it is sometimes out of necessity that only one educator attends the workshop and then shares what he or she learns with colleagues. The continuation of educators' professional growth and development in early STEM education beyond the introductory workshop depends on an established STEM learning community of practice.

4. The intensity and duration of the PD is matched to the content being conveyed. R&P professional development understands that because of the diverse scope of educational backgrounds and professional experiences that exist across the field of early childhood educators and child-care providers (as previously discussed), gauging the necessary intensity and instructional duration of the introductory workshop is difficult to achieve on an individual basis for all early childhood educators. For this reason, the introductory workshop is envisioned as providing a *foundation* for early STEM education, and the establishment of communities of practice enable educators to continue learning and applying what they learn in the workshop with colleagues as they implement R&P activities with young children.

5. Educators are prepared to conduct child assessments and interpret their results as a tool for ongoing monitoring of the effects of PD. R&P professional development recognizes the important role that assessment plays in the inquiry teaching process, as represented in the ITM. Assessment during R&P activities is based largely on teachers' recorded observations of what the child is able to do and understand, as informed by the child's decisions (as described elaborately in Chapter 7).

6. It is appropriate for the organizational context and aligned with standards for practice. R&P's early STEM activities are developmentally appropriate for children ages 3–8 years, and the corresponding R&P professional development has been developed for all early childhood professionals working with those age groups in a variety of settings. The challenge for workshop presenters, as mentioned earlier, is to adapt the content and activities as necessary to satisfy the background experiences, knowledge, and understanding of the different participants. R&P professional development is aligned with the *National Science Education Standards for Teaching* (NRC, 1996; see Figure 8.1) and the *Next Generation Science Standards* (as described throughout the guide).

Although significant progress has been made in attaining consensus regarding *what* (knowledge and skills) students should *learn* using scientific inquiry (as elaborated in Chapter 3), there is less agreement on *how* best to *instruct* students in science (Anderson, 2007) in order to achieve the desired learning outcomes. R&P professional development has been developed specifically to help address and satisfy this void in early STEM professional development.

Figure 8.1. *National Science Education Standards* **(NRC, 1996)**

TEACHING STANDARDS GRADES K–4		
Standard A	Standard B	Standard E
Teachers of science plan inquiry-based science programs	Teachers of science guide and facilitate learning	Teachers of science develop communities of science learners • Reflecting intellectual rigor of scientific inquiry • Reflecting attitudes and social values conducive to learning science

Introductory Workshop's Purpose

The 3-hour introductory R&P workshop, as described by Counsell, Uhlenberg, and Zan (2013), provides early educators with the information they need to begin implementing R&P activities in various educational settings that include public and private preschool programs, Head Start, center-based programs, home day care programs, and public and private primary grade classrooms. The purpose of the introductory training is to provide early educators with the opportunity to do the following:

- Explore and become familiar with the R&P materials (as described in detail in Chapter 2).
- Learn how to conduct explorations and investigations using R&P materials.
- Identify, manipulate, and control different variables (such as varying the ramp lengths, moving objects, and degree of slope) during R&P activities.
- Observe videos of teachers and children in real classrooms engaging with the R&P materials.
- Learn how to use the Inquiry Teaching Model (ITM) to guide and facilitate STEM instruction, children's learning, and development.
- Enhance teachers' observational and inquiry skills and strategies to support, enhance, and increase children's learning (see Photo 8.1).

R&P professional development challenges early childhood professionals to pay particular attention to (1) the role of teachers, (2) the role of learners, and (3) the use of authentic STEM activities and experiences to support STEM thinking, learning, and instruction. During an exploration activity, workshop participants working in small groups are encouraged to examine and play with three blocks or sponges, a 1-foot ramp section, a bucket, and miscellaneous objects (such as marbles, cotton balls, cubes, beads, and tops).

If necessary, participants are asked, "How do these objects roll down an incline?" After playing with the materials, participants describe how

Photo 8.1. Teachers Investigate During an Introductory R&P Workshop

they made an incline and are asked, "What happened as you released objects on the incline?" The workshop trainer circulates among the different groups and observes what participants do, makes comments, and asks probing questions that will challenge participants to think about what they are doing.

Participants share their observations and describe what happened with the objects they used during large-group discussion. Participants also identify which objects they didn't use and why they didn't use them.

STEM activities used during the introductory R&P workshop capitalize on authentic investigations and experimentations. Workshops are organized according to an adapted learning cycle (Cooney, Escalada, & Unruh, 2005), as described in Chapter 3. As workshop participants pursue their own goals, problems, and questions during investigations and experimentations, they change or control different variables (such as ramp height, length, and slope) in order to make predictions and formulate hypotheses about possible causal relationships.

Participants can further vary surface textures that the marble would make contact with upon exiting the final ramp (for example, wood, tile, or carpeted floors) to determine whether different surface textures affect the rate of speed or the distance the sphere travels. Participants can also compare how different objects move (spinning, rolling, or sliding) or whether an object's weight affects the distance it travels or its rate of speed. Teachers who want to investigate whether the variable of height affects the marble's rate of speed, for instance, would design and execute an experiment to determine any causal relationships. Workshop trainers guide and facilitate educators' application of STEM knowledge, concepts, and theory (such as Newton's Laws) to support their hypotheses, interpret the outcomes of their investigations, and inform future ramp structures in an ongoing, circular fashion (Counsell, 2011).

Introductory Workshop Content

As workshop participants actively engage in a series of activities (explorations, investigations, and experimentations) with R&P materials, small- and large-group discussions help participants identify, elaborate on, and expand on meanings, understanding, and relationships pertaining to the following STEM and teaching concepts and ideas (as defined and applied in previous chapters in this guide):

- Inquiry Teaching Model
- Fundamental role of observation during the inquiry teaching process
- Scientific distinctions between exploration, investigation, and experimentation
- Problem-solving process
- Various science process skills (e.g., observe, communicate, estimate, and so forth)
- Use of assessments to guide and inform STEM instruction and learning
- Implementation of productive questions to scaffold and support learning
- Constructivist theory
- Different STEM content and ideas (e.g., linear and rotational motion, Newton's Laws, work and energy, and so forth)
- Dependent and independent variables

The science terminology and concepts discussed and applied during R&P activities, though appropriate and desirable to enhance adult learners' understanding and scientific thinking, should be minimized or eliminated with young children, emphasizing practical relationships and applications instead (as explained in Chapter 3). For example, instead of referring to the marble's velocity or speed as it moves along the pathway, it would be more developmentally appropriate to simply ask, "How fast is the object moving?"

Emerging research reveals that the effects of training can fade over time, suggesting that in order for training to be effective, it needs to be ongoing, revisited, and renewed periodically (Burchinal, Cryer, Clifford, & Howes, 2002; Donovan, Bransford, & Pellegrino, 1999; Norris, 2001). After completing the introductory 3-hour workshop, early educators interested in implementing R&P with young children are strongly encouraged to establish a community of practice with other interested teachers within their workplace or nearby in order to continue participating in learning opportunities with colleagues using R&P.

SUSTAINING PROFESSIONAL DEVELOPMENT WITHIN SCIENCE COMMUNITIES OF PRACTICE

Communities of practice are professional learning groups designed to increase performance through collective work effort (Ingersoll, 2004; Wenger, 1998). Forming communities of practice enables professionals to work collaboratively on agreed-upon agendas in order to increase job performance through ongoing group support and feedback from participating community members. Early STEM communities of practice empower teachers as STEM learners and, ideally, as STEM leaders within the workplace.

The R&P curriculum and PD is aligned with the NRC's (2007) stance on science professional development. Effective PD requires ongoing collective efforts by various community members (teachers, developmental specialists, caregivers, children's museum personnel, administrators, and parents) within communities of practice.

EARLY STEM COMMUNITIES OF PRACTICE

Effective professional development requires ongoing opportunities to practice new concepts and skills. Communities of practice provide the ideal context for teachers to learn and practice new skills. These communities can

- Enable teachers to gather periodically
- Support continual exploration and investigation of materials
- Provide opportunities to learn science concepts and relationships on an ongoing basis
- Provide support as teachers learn how to implement R&P
- Foster collaboration among teachers to overcome potential barriers
- Allow teachers to grow together in their confidence as science learners

Although bringing people together to share ideas and experiences may be essential, simply forming groups of people to work together will not automatically guarantee the collaboration, cooperation, and support needed to increase learner outcomes, enhance teacher expertise, and improve teaching practice. Formulating and maintaining working groups alone may not increase teamwork or improve practice (McLaughlin & Talbert, 2000; Supovitz, 2002).

Remember to choose community members wisely. Be sure to form a community of practice with the members who share the same enthusiasm and vision for an improved early STEM experience for both learners and practitioners, while always leaving the door wide open for others to join at any time.

Considerations for Different Program Settings

Eventual classroom experiences by teachers and children will help showcase the potential learning and instructional outcomes experienced using R&P. It is important to keep an open invitation for other colleagues to visit classrooms as children are working with R&P or to attend STEM community meetings. Regardless of the members, it is essential for the group to have clear intentionality, vision, and an open willingness to support one another at the outset (NRC, 2007) as R&P is implemented with young children in educational settings.

An independent child-care provider who works alone may want to contact other child-care providers who might be equally interested in learning about and using R&P to enhance and support young children's scientific thinking. Local, state, or national agencies or organizations such as the state- or local-level Association for the Education of Young Children (AEYC) can help locate other providers in local areas who are interested in using R&P as early STEM enrichment activities. The Regents' Center for Early Developmental Education's R&P website (www.uni.edu/rampsandpathways) features teachers implementing R&P with young children. Regents' Center staff can also be contacted through the website for additional information and assistance.

As EC professionals identify colleagues interested in collaborating, it is equally imperative to include program supervisors or administrators (or other supportive agency administrators such as local child-care licensing coordinators) in the conversation early on to help recruit and support local efforts. If school or program administrators do not understand the learning and developmental benefits of R&P activities, they may fail to support and allow teachers to use them in their classrooms.

For example, one kindergarten teacher at a Reading First grant school was invited to participate in the R&P field testing. She emailed her principal regarding the prospect of serving as a participant and integrating

R&P into her classroom curriculum. She explained in her correspondence to her principal that the ramps would be available for children to use in a free-choice, center-type setting. She was a graduate student at the time, and she was learning about constructivist teaching practices. As a result of her coursework, she recognized the value and educational benefits that are afforded to children when they are allowed to explore and follow what interests them.

In spite of this teacher's constructive attempt to negotiate the curricular requirements of a Reading First school focus, her principal denied her (and ultimately, her students) the opportunity to participate in the R&P field testing. Her principal conceded that it was an honor to receive an invitation to participate. However, the principal consulted other school and district personnel and the consensus was to decline the offer. The principal cited time constraints, and questioned the alignment with standards and required time spent apart from students in order to complete the necessary training. The principal indicated to the teacher that she regretted how federal mandates have driven these kinds of decisions. This school district used a direct instruction model and, according to the principal, that approach was helping the district to address the mandates and achieve the designated goals.

As this scenario clearly illustrates, teachers need to share this guide with program administrators prior to participating in R&P workshops. This guide helps teachers explain R&P's efficacy, alignment with national and state early childhood guidelines and standards, and overall cost-effectiveness to increase early science learning outcomes while improving teaching practice in early science education. Topics and concerns, as illustrated above, may have particular interest and importance for program administrators.

Planning R&P Community Meetings

Establishing communities of practice empowered to improve and enrich science learning communities must include community meetings designed with a twofold purpose. First, to increase and expand on teachers' STEM knowledge and understanding, community members require ongoing opportunities to explore, investigate, and experiment with R&P activities and materials. Second, in order to continually enhance STEM teaching-learning experience through improved teaching practice, STEM community members must have the opportunity to openly share and discuss individual STEM teaching experiences and reflections using R&P with colleagues.

Logistics of meetings. Teachers who want to gather together to support one another will have to decide on the logistics of time, place, and frequency of meeting. In the R&P pilot and field studies, teachers gathered for monthly meetings of 2–3 hours each. However, this may not be possible for all groups, given teachers' schedules.

Agreeing on the same days (such as the second and fourth Tuesday of the month) and time to meet helps promote regular attendance. Most educators prefer meeting as a community of practice at the end of the school day. Classrooms where teachers are implementing R&P are ideal for meetings because these settings have readily available materials for use during the meetings. Rotating meetings to different locations enables different teacher participants to showcase the kinds of ramp structures children are building, different classroom arrangements used to accommodate ramp structures, and varied furniture and other materials used as ramp supports.

Science is a social enterprise. Science (as both a content and activity) is first and foremost a social enterprise. Any advancement of scientific theory or new discoveries relies on debate among scientists. Like children, adult science learners require a scientific learning community based on an open, actively engaged social context that encourages taking multiple perspectives, brainstorming, and the problem solving needed to increase scientific thinking, knowledge, and understanding. Adult learners need ongoing opportunities to actively participate in discussions while experimenting as STEM learners in order to conceptualize the educational benefits of this learning arrangement.

A variety of formats can be used to structure community meetings. One general format we have used during R&P community meetings and found to be quite effective in promoting our meetings as a democratic, social activity is organized into the following three general activity cycles in which teachers:

- share, reflect, perspective-take, and problem-solve;
- explore, investigate, experiment, and apply STEM concepts and relationships; and
- summarize gained insights and experiences concerning inquiry-based practice (using the ITM) to support young children's STEM learning.

R&P has the potential to not only transform early STEM programs and instruction but to transform professional teacher development in early STEM. In order to maximize PD, the community culture of practice must include activities that foster mentorship, teacher reflection, and support networks.

Mentoring science learners, explorers, investigators, and experimenters. Just as Akerson, Buzzelli, and Donnelly (2010) determined that the cooperating teacher was the most important factor influencing preservice teachers during early science instruction at the college level, the same can be said for early childhood practitioners within STEM learning communities. The central role that mentorship plays within PD cannot be overstated. Although it is true that educators working with any group of children can readily explore and learn about R&P on their own, it has been our experience that STEM learning is maximized when completed within social group settings. Mentorship, on the other hand, as suggested by Counsell (2011), "is an exclusively social activity" that cannot be achieved in isolation (p. 55). Becoming STEM mentors to children begins with becoming STEM mentors to colleagues within community cultures of practice.

During community meetings, teachers practice inquiry-based intervention strategies and skills with colleagues as they explore ramp materials, build ramp structures, and conduct investigations and experimentations during R&P activities (see Photo 8.2). Teachers can take turns observing and intervening with questions and comments, guiding and facilitating scientific thinking and understanding without telling or directing ramp builders' reasoning.

As noted earlier in this chapter, teachers will struggle to successfully implement inquiry teaching practice if they have not experienced inquiry practice as learners. A 2nd-grade teacher who struggled with developing her inquiry skills during the fall semester noted, "Questioning without leading is challenging" (2nd-grade teacher, personal communication, October 30, 2008). After implementing R&P with children for an entire year, the same teacher continued to resist the impulse to lead children, as she declared,

Photo 8.2. Teachers Practice Inquiry Strategies During R&P Professional Development

"Questioning is so important! Don't lead them too much! Learn to avoid telling them" (2nd-grade teacher, personal communication, May 7, 2009).

After reading the article about productive questioning by Martens (1999) during the fall semester, a teacher admitted:

> The pages on questioning are in my head. I think I'm doing it and then I read the article and realize I have so many preconceived notions. I need to learn to step back and trust that they will get there. Throughout the day—in everything I do—not just ramps! Learning to ask better questions—allowing them to learn more and trust more! (Kindergarten teacher, personal communication, March 19, 2009)

At the last community meeting, this same teacher commented again on her ongoing challenges with using productive questioning during R&P activities:

> Deciding when to ask questions—this is a very important piece and I'm still figuring it out. It is an ongoing process. Learning to step back and not keep harping on them. That's what we do without realizing it! (Kindergarten teacher, personal communication, May 7, 2009)

In the R&P pilot and field studies, experimental challenges were provided at every meeting to compel teachers to identify, address, and satisfy questions and problems they encountered during R&P investigations and experimentations.

These teachers acknowledged and understood what they needed to do to guide and facilitate children's scientific thinking during R&P activities, using the following five specific inquiry-based intervention strategies recommended by DeVries and Sales (2011):

- Ask for predictions
- Suggest new possibilities for experimentation
- Help children become more conscious of what they do
- Provide counterexamples when children's conclusions contain misconceptions
- Encourage children to wonder about physical causes

Even with ongoing support and guided practice, the teachers' hard work and effort to change their teaching practice was a continuous work in progress (see Chapter 2 for detailed discussion on questioning ideas and intervention).

Cumulative experiences constructing and revising ramp structures enable teachers to make better-informed decisions as ramp builders, constructing increasingly complex structures with various features such as corners, tunnels, fulcrums, catapults, and drops. Over time, teachers revise their self-image as competent STEM learners through newly gained understanding. This new self-image equips them to effectively guide and facilitate (mentor) young children's explorations and investigations. Active STEM learning experiences like those provided by R&P enable adult learners to revise and increase their understanding in an ongoing fashion, transforming them from capable adult STEM learners to increasingly competent STEM mentors, prepared to guide and facilitate both adult learners' and young children's scientific thinking, exploration, and investigation.

At the end of a yearlong journey of using R&P with her students, a 2nd-grade teacher decided to conduct her own experiment and share R&P with the other 2nd-grade classrooms to see what would happen. The 2nd-grade teaching team at her school switched for art, science, social studies, and creative writing. The teacher taught the core science lessons for the other 2nd-grade classes. At the last science community meeting, she shared the following:

> I took the ramps to different classrooms because I wanted to see what the other 2nd-graders would do. I used the ramps with the other classes for physical science. I talked to them about gravity, speed, and energy. We discussed the rules we follow when we use the ramps. It was amazing to see them start from scratch and to realize how far my own class has come—how far behind these students were in their understanding of gravity—so much further behind my kids. Students asked, "Can you come back with your ramps?" One little girl said, "This was the funnest [sic] thing we've done all year long!" These kids loved it! They thought they were in heaven. Recently when we switched classes again, it was time to start a unit on plants. I brought in seeds to use. All the students asked, "Where are the ramps?" They insisted, "We want ramps!" It only solidifies for us that there is something going on that kids benefit from! The day spent with ramps was the best day of the year according to some students. (2nd-grade teacher, personal communication, May 7, 2008)

This teacher's willingness to take R&P outside the security of her own classroom into other teachers' classrooms not only reflected her increased confidence and comfort level with her own STEM knowledge and understanding, but it meant that she was strategically poised to begin mentoring the inquiry approach and early STEM strategies with her colleagues. Helping teachers to first think scientifically, analyze phenomena, and engage in meaningful discourse with peers within STEM learning communities enables them to successfully connect STEM learning experiences in ways that ultimately reinvent STEM teaching practice (as indicated by this 2nd-grade teacher's experiences).

Identifying local STEM experts as potential mentors and resources, as described by Counsell, Peat, Vaughan, and Johnson (2015), can contribute significantly toward the group's overall professional development and teaching success. Outlets for locating local STEM experts include area high schools, community colleges, 4-year college institutions, and science museums.

Sharing teacher reflections. R&P professional development recognizes and supports (1) the importance of teacher beliefs, (2) the internal tensions teachers experience in the change process, (3) teacher reflection, and (4) the creation of interactive environments that place conceptual connections at the center of all group activity (Bryan & Abell, 1999; Gabriele & Joram, 2007; Goodenbour & Boody, n.d.; Parke & Coble, 1997). R&P professional development places a central focus on the power and need for ongoing teacher reflection during community meetings.

As both a professional and cultural activity within communities of practice, teacher reflection is an essential component of educators' need to change or readjust their beliefs, prior knowledge, skills, and eventual STEM teaching practice. Throughout this guide, the authors have shared inspiring teacher testimonials and reflections based on firsthand experiences implementing R&P with young children in educational settings. Altogether, these teacher reflections provide some of the most powerful and insightful evidence available to support the efficacy of R&P with young children.

Teachers need to share their firsthand experiences using R&P with young children on a regular basis. Teachers can record daily experiences using R&P in teacher journals and class portfolios. Other documents that can be shared with colleagues, administrators, and parents include the following:

- Student ramp drawings
- Student ramp writings
- Ramp charts, graphs, and tables
- Photos of children's ramp structures
- Videos of children constructing ramps

It is intrinsically motivating and emotionally rewarding for teachers to share their students' enthusiasm and accomplishments within communities of practice. On the other hand, it is equally important to openly discuss concerns, challenges, and possible frustrations while implementing R&P without feeling guilty, ashamed, embarrassed, or inadequate. One Head Start preschool teacher working with a Native American community was particularly frustrated with her efforts to entice children (3–5 years) to engage in R&P activities in the block area and reluctantly shared:

I'm still struggling to get the kids to experiment. Ramps are available all the time. I try to engage them. I start building a structure and ask children to help me build. They like glarch [goop] or playdough more. (January 22, 2009)

As the year progressed and the community members developed rapport, they openly offered suggestions to support one another's efforts. For example, other teachers suggested that the Head Start preschool teacher quoted above try using micro-cars to pique children's interest.

Open and honest discussions encourage and empower community members to negotiate, brainstorm, and problem-solve with their peers in order to develop new approaches. It wasn't until a year later that the preschool teacher working with a new group of preschoolers at the same Head Start program wrote in an email:

Guess what? I have the ramps in my classroom and the kids I have this year absolutely love them. They play with them—they even are now building ramps! I was so excited! Too bad I didn't have this bunch last year. (Head Start preschool teacher, personal communication, December 3, 2009)

Peer experts (possessing needed skills or competencies) can provide important peer-mediated intervention to novice learners (as described in Chapter 5). It cannot be presumed that the absence of expert "builders" asking questions and helping peers in the Head Start class to problem-solve and stimulate interest and scientific thinking alone resulted in less interest and engagement. Other contributing variables such as teaching style, teacher–child interactions, and class schedules must likewise be considered. Nonetheless, the role that experts play is noteworthy and should be researched in future studies that could further support the learning and instructional benefits and advantages that diversity can play in maximizing scientific thinking (and STEM learning in general) within natural (inclusive) settings.

Bringing teachers together to reflectively think and talk about their philosophical teaching and learning orientations and how these views guide, inform, and influence their teaching practice is an important aspect within the change process. Nonetheless, bringing community members to potentially question, challenge, and gain new understanding about their own beliefs in contrast to other members' beliefs will not guarantee that all community members will choose to revise their teaching approach or practices, as indicated by one Montessori preschool teacher:

Montessori is all individualized. When introducing R&P, it was important to establish rules first. Students could work with the materials either individually or in pairs. Everyone was getting into it and building more elaborate structures but it was getting so loud! Before the Christmas break it was getting really loud so I took them away. Montessori allows one child to work with materials at a time—sometimes pairs are allowed to work on ramps. I had to establish a one-person rule or a two-person rule—that's the Montessori learning environment. Loud and interrupting is not okay when children are completing Montessori work. (Montessori preschool teacher, personal communication, January 22, 2009)

Her effort to navigate the philosophical differences between the Montessori work cycle and the social context for STEM learning promoted during R&P resulted in her decision to limit children's access to R&P to the last hour of class on Fridays:

Ramps are now available Fridays only. Now we are able to get back into the Montessori routine—more structured again. Friday is usually different—fun stuff that day. We start ramps at 9:00 A.M. and go until 10:00 A.M. Before when it got too noisy, we had to put them away. Now I don't care how loud it gets—we're all doing it at the same time—instead of during work time. (Montessori preschool teacher, personal communication, March 19, 2009)

Her continued adherence to the Montessori approach meant she had to negotiate her schedule to allow for R&P whole-group activity apart from the Montessori curriculum. Teachers must be willing to examine and critique their philosophical views before they will be able to fully integrate a contrasting approach that will force them to revise their teaching practices.

Building networks of support. Once teachers have made the commitment to learn about and use R&P to enhance and improve the early STEM curriculum, it is equally important to recruit parental interest and support. Teachers can provide parents with information about R&P in newsletters, on program websites, on Twitter, or on a Facebook page. Valuable resources and materials are available at the Regents' Center R&P website (www.uni.edu/rampsandpathways/).

Parents can help with donations (either money or materials) or fundraisers to help purchase the necessary R&P supplies and materials. Contact local businesses and lumberyards regarding the possibility of making donations or providing discounts on needed materials. If a parent has a table saw and is willing to cut the cove molding into different lengths, this will help conserve funds.

Parents can further support teachers' efforts by asking their children about their experiences building ramps and releasing objects (What kind of ramp did you build? What could the marble do? How could you change it? What could you do differently?). R&P photos and children's drawings and writings can be shared as important evidence of children's learning and understanding (as described in Chapter 7) during parent–teacher conferences and during individualized education program (IEP) meetings with parents.

As children increase their confidence, abilities, creativity, and skills building ramp structures, learners can showcase their ramp structures at school events or build ramp structures with parents at a school parents' night or an open house:

> I planned a special parent–child literacy night for my kindergarten classes and included one activity with ramps. I enjoyed watching parents and their children interact during ramp building. Children are now going home and talking about it! How often do kids, when asked what they did in school today, say "Nothing"? Parents don't get that answer with ramps! (Kindergarten teacher, November 13, 2008)

Teachers can invite local news stations or newspapers to a program event highlighting R&P early physical science learning activities and experiences. Talk to your local chamber of commerce for advice and assistance on how best to approach business owners and recruit their support for your early science program.

R&P workshop training information is available through the University of Northern Iowa's Regents' Center for Early Developmental Education and can be accessed at the R&P website. Workshop presenters are available in geographic regions nationwide. For additional information, contact the Regents' Center at 319-273-2101.

SUSTAINING CHANGE

Current research on school reform and change in teacher practice has discussed many issues and considerations that must be addressed if change is to be sustained. New practices are not fixed but are continually modified and developed as teachers (adult learners) gain new knowledge and skills. It should be expected that participants undergoing change frequently experience discomfort and discontinuity. As a result, teachers require ongoing support from all levels to help them through the long, arduous, but most worthwhile process.

Though all schools are not yet equitable places for all children, according to Brooks (2011), they all can be. The R&P curriculum provides spaces of liberty and opportunities for free thought, as children solve problems and voice their perspectives and ideas. Cultures of practice promoted by R&P support liberty and empower educators as active learners, mentors, and problem-solvers prepared to implement inquiry-based explorations and investigations with young children. This, in turn, reinvents the role of teacher, learner, and science education for *everyone*.

References

Akerson, V. L. (2004). Designing a science methods course for early childhood preservice teachers. *Journal of Elementary Science Education, 16*(2), 19–32.

Akerson, V. L., Buzzelli, C. A., & Donnelly, L. A. (2010). On the nature of teaching nature of science: Preservice early childhood teachers' instruction in preschool and elementary settings. *Journal of Research in Science Teaching, 47*(2), 213–233.

Alderman, T. (2008). *Meeting the needs of your most able pupils: Science.* New York, NY: Routledge.

American Association for the Advancement of Science (AAAS). (1991). *Update project 2061.* Washington, DC: Author.

American Association for the Advancement of Science (AAAS). (1993). *Benchmarks for science literacy.* New York, NY: Oxford University Press.

Anderson, R. (2007). Inquiry as an organizing theme for science curricula. In S. Abell & N. Lederman (Eds.), *Handbook of research on science education* (pp. 807–830). Mahwah, NJ: Lawrence Erlbaum Associates.

Atwater, M. M. (1996). Social constructivism: Infusion into the multicultural science education research agenda. *Journal of Research in Science Teaching, 33*(8), 821–837.

Beneke, S. J. (2010). *The effects of the Project Approach on children in inclusive early childhood classrooms* (Unpublished dissertation). University of Illinois at Urbana-Champaign, Urbana, IL.

Berk, L., & Winsler, A. (1995). *Scaffolding children's learning: Vygotsky and early childhood education.* Washington, DC: National Association for the Education of Young Children.

Blair, C., & Razza, R. P. (2007). Relating effortful control, executive function, and false belief understanding to emerging math and literacy ability in kindergarten. *Child Development, 78*(2), 647–663.

Boardman, M. (2007). "I know how much this child has learned. I have proof!": Employing digital technologies for documentation processes in kindergarten. *Australian Journal of Early Childhood, 32*(3), 59–67.

Bone, J. (2001). Learning dispositions: Picking up the threads. *Australian Journal of Early Childhood, 26*(2), 25.

Bransford, J., Brown, A., & Cocking, R. (1999). *How people learn: Brain, mind, experience, and school.* Washington, DC: National Academy Press.

Brock, L. L., Rimm-Kaufman, S. E., Nathanson, L., & Grimm, K. J. (2009). The contributions of "hot" and "cool" executive function to children's academic achievement, learning-related behaviors, and engagement in kindergarten. *Early Childhood Research Quarterly, 24*(3), 337–349.

Brooks, J. G. (2011). *Big science for growing minds: Constructivist classrooms for young thinkers.* New York, NY: Teachers College Press.

Bryan, L. A., & Abell, S. K. (1999). The development of professional knowledge in learning to teach elementary science. *Journal of Research in Science Teaching, 36,* 121–139.

Burchinal, M. R., Cryer, D., Clifford, R. M., & Howes, C. (2002). Caregiver training and classroom quality in child care centers. *Applied Developmental Science, 6*(1), 2–11.

Bybee, R. (2013). *Translating the NGSS for classroom instruction.* Arlington, VA: National Science Teachers Association Press.

Capobianco, B. M., Yu, J. H., & French, B. F. (2014). Effects of engineering design-based science on elementary school science students' engineering identity development across gender and grade. *Research in Science Education. 45*(2), 275–292.

Carlisle, J. F., & Chang, V. (1996). Evaluation of academic capabilities in science by students with and without learning disabilities and their teachers. *The Journal of Special Education, 30*(1), 18–34.

Casey, B. M., Andrews, N., Schindler, H., Kersh, J. E., & Samper, A. (2008). The development of spatial skills through interventions involving block building activities. *Cognition and Instruction, 26,* 269–309.

Casey, M. B., Nuttal, R. L., & Pezaris, E. (1997). Mediators of gender differences in mathematics college entrance test scores: A comparison of spatial skills with internalized beliefs and anxieties. *Developmental Psychology, 33,* 669–680.

Cervetti, G. N., Pearson, P. D., Bravo, M. A., & Barber, J. (2006). Reading and writing in the service of inquiry-based science. In R. Douglas, M. P. Klentschy, & K. Worth (Eds.), *Linking science and literacy in the K–8 classroom* (pp. 221–244). Arlington, VA: NSTA Press.

Chalufour, I., & Worth, K. (2004). *Building structures with young children.* St. Paul, MN: Redleaf Press.

Clark, B. (2002). *Growing up gifted* (6th ed.). Upper Saddle River, NJ: Merrill Prentice Hall.

Clay, M. M. (2005). *Literacy lessons designed for individuals: Part two—teaching procedures.* Portsmouth, NH: Heinemann.

Cohen, L., & Uhry, J. (2007). Young children's discourse strategies during block play: a Bakhtinian approach. *Journal of Research in Childhood Education, 21*(3), 302.

Colangelo, N., & Davis, G. A. (Eds.). (1997). *Handbook of gifted education* (2nd ed.). Boston, MA: Allyn & Bacon.

Committee on Highly Successful Schools or Programs in STEM Education & National Research Council. (2011). *Successful K-12 STEM education: Identifying effective approaches in science, technology, engineering, and mathematics.* Washington, DC: National Academies Press.

Cook, R. E., Klein, M. D., & Tessier, A. (2008). *Adapting early childhood curricula for children with special needs.* Upper Saddle River, NJ: Pearson Education.

Cooney, T. M., Escalada, L. T., & Unruh, R. D. (2005). *PRISMS (Physics resources and instructional strategies for motivating students) PLUS.* Cedar Falls, IA: University of Northern Iowa Physics Department.

Cooney, T. M., Escalada, L. T., & Unruh, R. D. (2008). *Physics resources and instructional strategies for motivating students (PRISMS) PLUS.* Cedar Falls, IA: University of Northern Iowa.

Council of Chief State School Officers. (2011). *InTASC Model Core Teaching Standards: A resource for state dialogue.* Retrieved from www.ccsso.org/Documents/2011/InTASC_Model_Core_Teaching_Standards_2011.pdf

Counsell, S. (2009, Summer). Abandoning the least restrictive environment in favor of natural settings: The achievement of social justice for all—It's a right not a privilege! *The Constructivist, 20*(1), 1–30, ISSN 1091-4072.

Counsell, S. (2011). Becoming science "experi-mentors"—Tenets of quality professional development and how they can reinvent early science learning experiences. *Science & Children, 49*(2), 52–56.

Counsell, S., Peat, F., Vaughan, R., & Johnson, J. (2015). Inventing mystery machines! Collaborating to improve teacher STEM preparation. *Science & Children, 52*(7), 64–70.

Counsell, S., Uhlenberg, J., & Zan, B. (2013). Ramps and Pathways early physical science program: Preparing educators as science mentors. In S. Koba and B. Wognowskit (Eds.), *Exemplary science: Best practices in professional development* (pp. 143–156). Arlington, VA: National Science Teachers Association Press.

DeVries, R., & Kohlberg, L. (1990). *Constructivist early education: Overview and comparison with other programs.* Washington, DC: National Association for the Education of Young Children. (Original work published 1987)

DeVries, R., & Sales, C. (2011). *Ramps & Pathways: A constructivist approach to physics with young children.* Washington, DC: National Association for the Education of Young Children.

DeVries, R., & Zan, B. (1994). *Moral classrooms, moral children: Creating a constructivist atmosphere in early education.* New York, NY: Teachers College Press.

DeVries, R., & Zan, B. (2012). *Moral classrooms, moral children: Creating a constructivist atmosphere in early education* (2nd ed.). New York, NY: Teachers College Press.

Diamond, A. (2013). Executive functions. *Annual Review of Psychology, 64*, 135–168. doi: 10.1146/annurev-psych-113011-143750

Diamond, A., Barnett, W. S., Thomas, J. & Munro, S. (2007). Preschool program improves cognitive control. *Science, 318*(5855), 1387–1388.

Diamond, J. (2005). *Collapse: Societies choose to fail or succeed.* New York, NY: Penguin.

Division of Early Childhood (DEC). (2007). *Promoting positive outcomes for children with disabilities: Recommendations for curriculum, assessment, and program evaluation.* Missoula, MT: Author.

Dodge, D. T., Colker, L. J., & Heroman, C. (2002). *The creative curriculum for preschool* (4th ed.). Washington, DC: Teaching Strategies.

Donovan, M. S., Bransford, J. D., & Pellegrino, J. W. (Eds.). (1999). *How people learn: Bridging research and practice.* Washington, DC: National Academies Press.

Duke, N. (2000). 3.6 minutes per day: The scarcity of informational texts in first grade. *Reading Research Quarterly, 35*(2), 202–224.

Elstgeest, J. (2001). The right question at the right time. In W. Harlen (Ed.), *Primary science: Taking the plunge* (2nd ed., pp. 25–35). Portsmouth, NH: Heinemann.

Fawcett, L. M., & Garton, A. F. (2005). The effect of peer collaboration on children's problem solving ability. *British Journal of Educational Psychology, 75*(2), 157–169.

Feynman, R. (1985). "Surely you're joking, Mr. Feynman!" Adventures of a curious character. New York, NY: W. W. Norton & Company.

Fitzgerald, L., & Dengler, R. (2010, May 4). *Use of productive questions by preservice teachers in early-childhood classrooms.* Paper presented at the annual meeting of the American Educational Research Association, Denver, CO.

Fox-Turnbull, W. (2010). The role of conversation in technology education. *Design and Technology Education: An International Journal, 15*(1).

Fradd, S. H., & Lee, O. (1995). Science for all: A promise or a pipe dream for bilingual students. *The Bilingual Research Journal, 19*(2), 261–278.

Fredericks, A. D., & Cheesebrough, D. L. (1998). *Science for all children: Elementary school methods.* Prospect Heights, IL: Waveland Press.

Gabriele, A. J., & Joram, E. (2007). Teachers' reflections on their reform-based teaching in mathematics: Implications for the development of teacher self-efficacy. *Action in Teacher Education, 29*(3), 60–74.

Gamire, E., & Pearson, G. (Eds.). (2006). *Tech tally: Approaches to assessing technological literacy.* Washington, DC: National Academies Press.

Geiken, R., Van Meeteren, B., & Kato, T. (2009). Putting the cart before the horse: The role of a socio-moral atmosphere in an inquiry-based curriculum. *Childhood Education, 85*(4), 4.

Gersten, R., & Baker, S. (1998). Real world use of scientific concepts: Integrating situated cognition with explicit instruction. *Exceptional Children, 65*(1), 23–35.

Gestwicki, C. (2007). *Developmentally appropriate practice: Curriculum and development in early education.* Clifton Park, NY: Thomson Delmar Learning.

Goodenbour, C. V., & Boody, R. M. (n.d.). The development of student self-assessment in the context of a fourth-grade literacy classroom. Manuscript submitted for publication.

Graves, D. H. (1994). *A fresh look at writing*. Portsmouth, NH: Heinemann.

Greenfield, D., Jirout, J., Dominguez, X., Greenberg, A., Maier, M., & Fuccillo, J. (2009). Science in the preschool classroom: A programmatic research agenda to improve science readiness. *Early Education and Development, 20*(2), 238–264.

Harlen, W. (Ed.). (2001). *Primary science: Taking the plunge* (2nd ed.). Portsmouth, NH: Heinemann.

Hart, B., & Risley, T. R. (2003). The early catastrophe: The 30 million word gap by age 3. *American Educator, 22*, 4–9.

Head Start Child Development and Early Learning Framework. (2010). Retrieved from eclkc.ohs.acf.hhs.gov/hslc/tta-system/teaching/eecd/Assessment /Child%20Outcomes/HS_Revised_Child_Outcomes_Framework%28rev -Sept2011%29.pdf

Howe, A. C. (2002). *Engaging children in science*. Upper Saddle River, NJ: Merrill Prentice Hall.

Ingersoll, R. E. (2004). *Who controls teachers' work? Power and accountability in America's schools*. Cambridge, MA: Harvard University Press.

International Technology and Engineering Educators Association (ITEEA). (2007). *Standards for technological literacy*. Reston, VA: Author.

Johnston, P. H. (2012). *Opening minds: Using language to change lives*. Portland, ME: Stenhouse Publishers.

Jones, J. (2011). Assessing young children's learning and development. *Principal, 90*(5), 12–15.

Kallery, M., & Psillos, D. (2001). Preschool teacher's content knowledge in science: Their understanding of elementary science concepts and of issues raised by children's questions. *International Journal of Early Years Education, 9*(3). doi:10.1080/09669760120086929

Kame'enui, E. J., Carnine, D., Dixon, R., Simmons, D., & Coyne, M. (2002). *Effective teaching strategies that accommodate diverse learners*. Upper Saddle River, NJ: Merrill/Prentice Hall.

Kamii, C., Miyakawa, Y., & Kato, Y. (2004). The development of logico-mathematical knowledge in a block-building activity at ages 1–4. *Journal of Research in Childhood Education, 19*(1), 44–45.

Karmiloff-Smith, A., & Inhelder, B. (1974). "If you want to get ahead, get a theory." *Cognition, 3*, 195–212.

Katehi, L., Pearson, G., & Feder, M. (2009). The status and nature of K–12 engineering education in the United States. *The bridge: Linking engineering and society, 39*(3), 5–10.

Kato, T., & Van Meeteren, B. (2008). Physical science in constructivist early childhood classrooms. *Childhood Education, 84*(4), 234–236.

Katz, L. G., & Chard, S. C. (1996). The contribution of documentation to the quality of early childhood education. *ERIC Digest*. Retrieved from www .ericdigests.org/1996-4/quality.htm

Katz, L. G., & Chard, S. C. (2000). *Engaging children's minds: The project approach*: Norwood, NJ: Ablex Publishing.

Keeley, P. (2008). *Science formative assessment—75 practical strategies for linking assessment, instruction, and learning.* Thousand Oaks, CA: Corwin Press/ NSTA Press.

Keen, R. (2010). The development of problem solving in young children: A critical cognitive skill. *Annual Review of Psychology, 62*, 1–21.

Kersh, J., Casey, B. M., & Young, J. M. (2008). Research on spatial skills and block building in girls and boys: The relationship to later mathematics learning. *Contemporary perspectives on mathematics in early childhood education*, 233–251.

Kliewer, C. (1998). The meaning of inclusion. *Mental Retardation, 36*(4), 317–322.

Knight, R. (2004). *Five easy lessons: Strategies for successful physics teaching.* San Francisco, CA: Addison Wesley.

Kuhn, M., & McDermott, M. (2013). Negotiating the way to inquiry. *Science and Children, 50*(9), 52–57.

Lan, X., Legare, C. H., Ponitz, C. C., Li, S., & Morrison, F. J. (2011). Investigating the links between components of executive function and academic achievement. *Journal of Experimental Child Psychology, 108*(3), 677–692. Retrieved from www.sciencedirect.com/science/article/pii/S0022096510002122#bb0190

Lawson, A. (2010). *Teaching inquiry science in middle and secondary schools.* Thousand Oaks, CA: Sage Publications.

Martens, M. L. (1999). Productive questions: Tools for supporting constructivist learning. *Science and Children, 36*(8), 24–27, 53–56.

Marx, R. W., & Harris, C. J. (2006). No child left behind and science education: Opportunities, challenges, and risks. *Elementary School Journal, 106*(5), 467–478.

Mashburn, A. J., Justice, L. M., Downer, J. T., & Pianta, R. C. (2009). Peer effects on children's language achievement during pre-kindergarten. *Child Development, 80*, 686–702.

Massachusetts Department of Education. (2013). *Massachusetts science and technology/engineering standards (draft).* Malden, MA: Author. Retrieved from www.doe.mass.edu/stem/standards/standardsdraft.pdf

McAfee, O., Leong, D. J., & Bodrova, E. (2004). *Basics of assessment: A primer for early childhood educators.* Washington, DC: NAEYC.

McClelland, M. M., Cameron, C. E., Wanless, S., & Murray, A. (2007). Executive function, behavioral self-regulation, and social-emotional competence: Links to school readiness. In O. N. Saracho & B. Spodek (Eds.), *Contemporary perspectives in early childhood education: Social learning in early childhood education, Vol. 7* (pp. 113–117). Greenwich, CT: Information Age.

McDermott, L. C. (1991). Millikan lecture 1990: What we teach and what is learned—closing the gap. *American Journal of Physics, 59*(4), 301–315.

McLaughlin, M., & Talbert, J. (2000). *Assessing results: The Bay Area school reform collaborative, year four.* Palo Alto, CA: Center for Research on the Context of Teaching, Stanford University.

Mol, S. E., & Neuman, S. B. (2014). Sharing information books with kindergartners: The role of parents' extra-textual talk and socioeconomic status. *Early Childhood Research Quarterly, 29*(4), 399–410.

Moll, L. (1992). *Vygotsky and education: Instructional implications and applications of sociohistorical psychology.* New York, NY: Teachers College Press.

National Academy of Sciences. (2007). *Rising above the gathering storm: Energizing and employing America for a brighter economic future.* Washington, DC: National Academies Press.

National Association for the Education of Young Children (NAEYC). (2009). *Where we stand on curriculum, assessment, and program evaluation.* Retrieved from www.naeyc.org/files/naeyc/file/positions/StandCurrAss.pdf

National Association for the Education of Young Children (NAEYC). (2014). *Early childhood program standards and accreditation criteria.* Washington, DC: NAEYC. Retrieved from www.naeyc.org/academy/files/academy/file/AllCriteriaDocument.pdf

National Center for Education Statistics. (2011). *The nation's report card: Science 2009* (NCES 2011-451). Institute of Education Sciences, U.S. Department of Education, Washington, DC: Author.

National Child Care Information and Technical Assistance Center. (2011). *State requirements for minimum preservice qualifications and annual ongoing training hours for child care center teachers and master teachers in 2011.* Retrieved from occarchive.org/pubs cclicensingreq/ccir-teachers.html

National Council of Teachers of Mathematics. (2000). *Principles and standards for school mathematics.* Reston, VA: Author.

National Governors Association Center for Best Practices & Council of Chief State School Officers. (2010a). *Common Core State Standards for English language arts & literacy in history/social studies, science, and technical subjects.* Retrieved from www.corestandards.org/wp-content/uploads/ELA_Standards.pdf

National Governors Association Center for Best Practices & Council of Chief State School Officers. (2010b). *Common Core State Standards for mathematics.* Retrieved from www.corestandards.org/wp-content/uploads/Math_Standards.pdf

National Institute of Child Health and Human Development—Early Child Care Research Network. (2005). A day in third grade: a large-scale study of classroom quality and teacher and student behavior. *Elementary School Journal, 105,* 305–323.

National Research Council (NRC). (1996). *National Science Education Standards.* Washington D.C.: National Academy Press.

National Research Council (NRC). (2001). *Eager to learn: Educating our preschoolers.* Washington, DC: National Academies Press.

National Research Council (NRC). (2007). *Taking science to school: Learning and teaching science in grades K–8.* Washington, DC: National Academies Press.

National Research Council (NRC). (2008). *Ready, set, science! Putting research to work in K–8 science classrooms.* Washington, DC: National Academies Press.

National Research Council (NRC). (2009). *Engineering in K–12 education.* Washington, DC: National Academies Press.

National Research Council (NRC). (2012). *A framework for K–12 science education*. Washington, DC: National Academies Press.

National Research Council (NRC). (2013). *Next generation science standards*. Washington, DC: National Academies Press.

Norris, D. J. (2001). Quality of care offered by providers with differential patterns of workshop participation. *Child and Youth Care Forum, 30*(2), 111–121.

Office of Head Start. (2011). *Head Start child development and early learning framework*. Arlington, VA: Head Start Resource Center.

Ostlund, K. (1992). *Science process skills—Assessing hands-on student performance*. Menlo Park, CA: Addison-Wesley.

Padilla, M. J., Muth, K. D., & Lund Padilla, R. (1991). Science and reading: Many process skills in common. *Science learning—Processes and applications*, 14–19.

Parke, H. M., & Coble, C. R. (1997). Teachers designing curriculum as professional development: A model for transformational science teaching. *Journal of Research in Science Teaching, 34*, 773–789.

Perret-Clermont, A. N. (1980). *Social interaction and cognitive development in children*. London, England: Academic Press.

Piaget, J. (1923/1959). *The language and thought of the child*. London, England: Routledge & Kegan Paul.

Piaget, J. (1960). *The child's conception of geometry*. London, England: Routledge and Kegan Paul. (Original work published 1948)

Piaget, J. (1965). *The moral judgment of the child*. New York, NY: Free Press.

Piaget, J. (with R. Garcia) (1974). *Understanding causality*. New York, NY: Norton. (Original work published 1971)

Piaget, J. (1973). *To understand is to invent: The future of education*. New York, NY: Grossman.

Piaget, J. (1978). *Success and understanding*. Cambridge, MA: Harvard University Press. (Original work published 1974)

Piaget, J. (1981). *Intelligence and affectivity*. Palo Alto, CA: Annual Reviews Inc.

Pianta, R., La Paro, K. M., & Hamre, B. K. (2008). *Classroom Assessment Scoring System: Manual, PreK*. Baltimore, MD: Paul H. Brookes.

President's Council of Advisors on Science and Technology (PCAST). (2010). *Prepare and inspire: K–12 education in science, technology, engineering, and math (STEM) for America's future*. Retrieved from www.whitehouse.gov/sites/default/files/microsites/ostp/pcast-stemed-report.pdf

Puckett, M. B., & Black, J. K. (2000). *Authentic assessment of the young child: Celebrating development and learning* (2nd ed.). Upper Saddle River, NJ: Merrill.

Raizen, S. (1988). *Increasing education productivity through improving the science curriculum*. Washington, DC: National Center for Improving Science Education.

Rapp, W. H. (2005). Inquiry-based environments for the inclusion of students with exceptional learning needs. *Remedial and Special Education, 26*(5), 297–310.

Robertson, W. (2002). *Force & motion and energy. Stop faking it! Finally understanding science so you can teach it.* Arlington, VA: NSTA Press.

Rose, D. H., & Meyer, A. (2002). *Teaching every student in the Digital Age: Universal design for learning.* Alexandria, VA: Association for Supervision and Curriculum Development (ASCD).

Sandholtz, J. H., & Ringstaff, C. (2011). Reversing the downward spiral of science instruction in K–2 classrooms. *Journal of Science Teacher Education, 22,* 513–533.

Seitz, H. (2008). The power of documentation in the early childhood classroom. *Young Children, 63*(2), 6.

Shaul, S., & Schwartz, M. (2014). The role of the executive functions in school readiness among preschool-age children. *Reading & Writing, 27*(4), 749.

Siegel, D. J. (2001). *The developing mind: How relationships and the brain interact to shape who we are.* New York, NY: Guilford Press.

Siry, C., Ziegler, G., & Max, C. (2012). "Doing science" through discourse-in-interaction: Young children's science investigations at the early childhood level. *Science Education 96*(2), 311–326.

Skamp, K., & Mueller, A. (2001). Student teachers' conceptions about effective elementary science teaching: A longitudinal study. *International Journal of Science Education, 23,* 331–351.

Spooner, F., DiBiase, W., & Courtade-Little, G. (2006). Science standards and functional skills. In D. M. Browder & F. Spooner (Eds.), *Teaching language arts, math, & science to students with significant cognitive disabilities* (pp. 229–243). Baltimore, MD: Paul H. Brookes.

Stoddart, T., Connell, M., Stofflett, R., & Peck, D. (1993). Reconstructing elementary teacher candidates' understanding of mathematics and science content. *Teacher & Teacher Education, 9*(3), 229–241.

Sullenger, K. (1999). How do you know science is going on? *Science and Children, 36*(7), 22–26.

Supovitz, J. (2002). Developing communities of instructional practice. *Teachers College Record, 104*(8), 1591–1626.

U.S. Bureau of Labor Statistics, Division of Occupational Employment Statistics. (2014). *May 2014 national occupational employment and wage estimates United States.* Retrieved from www.bls.gov/oes/home.htm

U.S. Department of Education, Office of Planning, Evaluation and Policy Development, Policy and Program Studies Service. (2010). *Toward the identification of features of effective professional development for early childhood educators, literature review.* Washington, DC: Author.

Van Meeteren, B. D., & Escalada, L. T. (2010). Science and literacy centers. *Science and Children, 47*(7), 74–78.

Van Meeteren, B., & Zan, B. (2010). Revealing the work of young engineers in early childhood education. *Early Childhood Research and Practice, 12*(2). Retrieved from ecrp.uiuc.edu/beyond/seed/index.html

Van Meeteren, B. D. (2013). *Engineering education from the perspective of the child* (Unpublished dissertation). University of Northern Iowa, Cedar Falls, IA.

Van Meeteren, B. D. (2014). *Ramps and pathways observational records* (Unpublished manuscript). Cedar Falls, IA: University of Northern Iowa.

Varelas, M., Kane, J. M., & Wylie, C. D. (2011, April). *Young black children and science: Chronotopes in their narratives around their science journals.* Paper presented at annual conference of the National Association for Research in Science Teaching, Orlando, FL.

Victor, E., Kellough, R. D., & Tai, R. H. (2008). *Science K–8: An integrated approach* (11th ed.). Upper Saddle River, NJ: Pearson Education.

Vygotsky, L. (1978). Interaction between learning and development. In L. Vygotsky, *Mind in society.* Cambridge, MA: Harvard University Press. (Original work published 1938)

Wenger, E. (1998). *Communities of practice: Learning, meaning, and identity.* New York, NY: Cambridge University Press.

Wenner, G. (1993). Relationship between science knowledge levels and beliefs toward science instruction held by preservice and elementary teachers. *Journal of Science Education and Technology, 2*(3), 461–468.

Willard-Holt, C. (1999). *Dual exceptionalities.* Reston, VA: ERIC Digest E574, ERIC Clearinghouse on Disabilities and Gifted Education.

Wilson, R. (n.d.). Promoting the development of scientific thinking. *Early childhood news.* Retrieved from www.earlychildhoodnews.com/earlychildhood /article_pront.aspx?ArticleId=409

Wolfgang, C. H., Stannard, L. L., & Jones, I. (2001). Block play performance among preschoolers as a predictor of later school achievement in mathematics. *Journal of Research in Childhood Education, 15*, 173–180.

Yasar, S., Baker, D., Robinson-Kurpius, S., Krause, S., & Roberts, C. (2006). Development of a survey to assess K–12 teachers' perceptions of engineers and familiarity with teaching design, engineering, and technology. *Journal of Engineering Education, 95*(3), 205–216.

Yore, L. D., Bisanz, G. L., & Hand, B. M. (2003). Examining the literacy component of science literacy: 25 years of language arts and science research. *International Journal of Science Education, 25*(6), 689–725.

Index

The letter *f* or *p* after a page number indicates a figure or photo, respectively.

About the Authors

Shelly Lynn Counsell, EdD, is an assistant professor of early childhood education at the University of Memphis and teaches the Planning and Facilitating Math and Science course. She was the southeast Idaho R&P site facilitator and a research fellow at the UNI Regents' Center. She has presented R&P and other early science workshops locally, nationally, and internationally. She coauthored an R&P chapter in NSTA's *Exemplary Science* PD text and has published articles in *Science & Children, Young Children, Schools: Studies in Education, Journal of Disability Policy Studies,* and *EPAA.* National presentations include National Science Teachers Association, National Association for the Education of Young Children, Association for Childhood Education International, Association for Constructivist Teaching, and American Education Research Association.

Lawrence Escalada, PhD, is a professor of physics and science education and chair of science education at the University of Northern Iowa. He has taught high school physics and now teaches university introductory physics and physical science courses (including those for elementary teaching majors) as well as secondary science methods courses. His research involves developing curricula including PRISMS PLUS and facilitating professional development for pre-K–12 teachers in addition to providing outreach opportunities for K–12 students. He collaborated with the coauthors and others in the development of R&P and helped facilitate related professional development for teachers.

Rosemary Geiken, EdD, is an associate professor of early childhood at East Tennessee State University. She has been in education for over 30 years, serving as a classroom teacher, early childhood consultant, center director, and university faculty. She was a research associate with the Regents' Center during the development of R&P. As a member of the R&P team she visited teachers who were implementing R&P, provided workshops on R&P, and facilitated meetings of the national field site leaders. She has presented nationally and internationally on physical science and young children. Her current research focuses on toddlers and problem solving.

Melissa Sander, MAE, is a special education teacher serving students ages 3 through 6th grade at Wapsie Valley Community School District in Iowa.

She has taught for 19 years in the field of special education and has used R&P within her classroom for academic instruction to meet IEP needs. She also leads R&P afterschool enrichments for heterogeneous groups of students in grades K–6. She has presented at local, state, and national conferences in the field of early childhood education, inclusion, and R&P. Her current focus is using R&P with school-age children to extend their reasoning skills.

Jill Uhlenberg, PhD, is an associate professor of early childhood education and head of the Department of Curriculum and Instruction at the University of Northern Iowa. She has a 30-year EC career as a teacher, center director, accreditation validator and commissioner, and teacher preparation faculty member. She teaches undergraduate and graduate courses for preservice and inservice teachers, with an integrated curriculum development focus, especially science and mathematics for young children. Her research includes toddler spatial problem solving through the Center for Early Education in STEM (CEESTEM), and she coauthored an R&P chapter in NSTA's *Exemplary Science* PD text.

Beth Van Meeteren, EdD, is director of the Regents' Center for Early Developmental Education and the Center for Early Education in STEM at the University of Northern Iowa. A veteran 1st-grade teacher, Van Meeteren developed early childhood STEM curricula that integrated literacy and assisted Dr. Rheta DeVries in research by translating the theory of cognitive development into classroom practice. Van Meeteren's own research emphasis is on early engineering within STEM and she has given numerous state, national, and international presentations and keynotes on early childhood STEM. She has published articles and is working on other book chapters on early STEM education.

Sonia Yoshizawa, MAE, is a doctoral fellow in the early childhood education program at East Tennessee State University. She formerly served as a research associate at the University of Northern Iowa. During the Ramps and Pathways project, she helped create interview protocols with Rheta DeVries and conducted pre- and posttest interviews for pre-K to 2nd-grade children in Iowa, Idaho, Alabama, and Texas. She has served as a STEM teacher trainer, instructor, director at the U.S. Embassy pre-K school, and pre-K and kindergarten teacher in Japan. She is the co-author of a book (in-press) on topics related to young children's creativity. She has presented nationally and internationally at major national conferences.

Betty Zan has a PhD in developmental psychology from the University of Houston. She serves as associate professor at the University of Northern Iowa, where she teaches classes in early childhood education. Dr. Zan is the coauthor of two books with the late Rheta DeVries (*Moral Classrooms,*

Moral Children and *Developing Constructivist Curriculum*). She served as principal investigator on the Ramps and Pathways project (funded by the National Science Foundation), which serves as the foundation for this book. She has presented on early STEM education nationally and internationally, and is a regular presenter at NAEYC.